Beyond the Lemonade Stand

14 Undergraduate Entrepreneurs
Tell Their Stories of Ethics in Business

COMPILED BY MICHAEL McMYNE
EDITED BY NICOLE AMARE, Ph.D.

Beyond the Lemonade Stand: 14 Undergraduate
Entrepreneurs Tell Their Stores of Ethics in Business

Compiled by Michael McMyne
Edited by Nicole Amare, Ph.D.

Published by Saint Louis University
Designed by Buisson Creative Strategies, Metairie, LA

ISBN 0-9761958-0-1
Library of Congress Catalog Number: 2004113330

First Edition 2004
1 2 3 4 5 6 7 8 9 10

We dedicate this book to
budding business leaders across the globe.
As you enter the environment of the
entrepreneur, may you find success that is
personally gratifying, intellectually challenging,
emotionally uplifting, and financially satisfying.
And may you serve as an inspiration to those around you.

Content

Foreword

Congratulations! You have begun a journey toward achieving your dream of becoming a business owner. This book will give you the tools and resources necessary to take your business idea to the next level. Chances are you are eager, excited, optimistic, and cautious as you begin your journey, as you navigate a path filled with triumph and excitement.

This book is a tool that will take you on a journey that students, just like you, took to achieve their dream of owning and operating a business. The case studies you will read will inspire you to take action and help you begin to develop a business plan. The students profiled in this tome are the globe's most recognized student business owners, so learn from their mistakes and benefit from their successes. As you read their story of hard work and dedication, notice their unyielding commitment to being ethical business owners. Also, recognize their drive, dedication, and desire to fulfill their lifelong dreams to be successful and ethical business owners. Let their stories inspire you to buckle up and take the ride of your life!

Just two years ago, I was lucky enough to be recognized as the Global Student Entrepreneur for Social Impact -- an award that I will forever cherish and appreciate. The recognition opened new doors for me and allowed for incredible networking opportunities. Sharon Bower's commitment to this program has allowed students across the globe to be recognized for their creativity, social impact, and entrepreneurial spirit. Her work has begun a revolution on college campuses, and she has only just begun! The Global Student Entrepreneur[SM] Awards are the most prestigious awards for undergraduate business owners, and this book recounts the success stories of those student entrepreneurs who are winners of these prestigious awards.

Probably the most important element you should extract from this book is the need for ethics. All of the authors in this book have realized that, as business owners, good business ethics is the most important part of their personal and professional lives. This respect is especially refreshing to hear from young business owners, particularly during a period in history where business is becoming synonymous with corruption, greed, and dishonesty. These student winners understand, above all else, that the future of global entrepreneurship is one that stems from hard work and honesty. I hope that you the reader -- a current or future entrepreneur yourself -- may glean this ethical lesson from these pages, and by doing so start a foundation of ethical business practices for others around you to follow. So, embrace these stories for both the economic and moral advice they have to offer, and you will find yourself and your business riding high, happy, and with honor.

--Michael J. McMyne

Acknowledgments

I have been blessed to meet and work with so many wonderful and dedicated people throughout this entire project. Their work and commitment was vital in the production of this book; moreover, without their support, I would never have begun my journey. Many of them deserve special recognition:

First and foremost to Sharon Bower, a friend, mentor and genius, whose vision and energy inspires me on a daily basis -- you are the spark that has ignited the fire in each student profiled herein;

To Ron Rubin, whose unending support and generosity allowed this book series to exist. I cherish your friendship and appreciate your guidance;

To Leah Kruger, whose wisdom and creativity guide this ship we are all on;

To Jeanne Rhodes, who puts up with me on a daily basis. Thanks for taking the calls and making the impossible possible;

To the Global Student Entrepreneur[SM] Awards Regional Partners, for your hard work and dedication in selecting the winners each year;

To our sponsors, for your generosity and support in helping recognize the award winning student entrepreneurs;

To my family, for teaching me that I can achieve whatever I set out to achieve. Especially to my mother and father for being my biggest fans and the best cheerleaders ever;

To Nicole Amare, our editor and my dear friend, for being a great partner and supporter. Thank you for standing by me and never saying no;

To Greg Buisson and the staff at Buisson Creative Strategies, for doing such a great job with our book design;

To Gina Amador, for the gorgeous and unique cover design;

To our printer, Pat Garrity, for your patience and understanding;

To Mike McCrossen, whose guidance got me started with all of this! Thank you for recognizing my potential and encouraging me to follow my dreams;

To the Alsfeld Family, who have inspired me in more ways than they will ever know. Your friendship is a blessing;

To Dr. Patricia Mark, who kept me positive when things started to get rough. You are a true "teacher";

To the brothers of the Delta Delta Zeta of Lambda Chi Alpha, who put up with my commitment to business and writing during the critical times;

To the faculty, staff, and administration at Spring Hill College, especially Karen Edwards, Fr. Michael Williams, SJ, and Dr. Noreen Carrocci, Ph.D., for encouraging me to believe in myself and dream big dreams. Thank you for putting up with me;

To Don Shiell whose mentoring and friendship has taken me places I only dreamed of going;

To Ron Sancho and his team at KOS -- thank you for taking a chance on me;

And last but not least, to LeeMarie, my pillar of support and my best friend. Thank you for standing by me and supporting me in everything I do. I love you.

--Michael J. McMyne

Preface

OW! Our second book in the Student Entrepreneur series, written by Regional Winners of the Global Student Entrepreneur[SM] Awards (GSEA). As the creator and Director of the Awards, I feel like the proud parent watching my progeny succeed. Forgive me if I strut like a peacock (or rather, like a peahen to be gender correct) as I look at what the winners of the Global Student Entrepreneur[SM] Awards have accomplished.

With the publishing of this second book, we now have a stable of 28 GSEA Regional Winners who are published authors. When these undergraduate entrepreneurs first applied for the Global Awards, they had no idea they would go beyond their existing entrepreneurial career to yet another career -- that of author! In fact, only one of the 28 was an "official" author before the books. I know that previously all of them had written countless term papers and reports, but those do not an author make!

This book differs slightly from the first one. After reading numerous articles in newspapers and magazines on the topic of business ethics (or should I say the lack of business ethics), I determined that by concentrating the second book on ethics, we could contribute to raising the level of standards and moral business behavior, by demonstrating that students do take ethics seriously as they launch and run their enterprises. We would show that ethics is good business!

So here we proudly are, with two books under our belt. And, Michael McMyne, you did it! The idea of the GSEA winners writing a book was all yours back at the 2002 awards in Washington DC. You believed it could be done, and by your dedication, we now have a set of books, with a third yet to be written. You have been a dynamo to work with and have made each day an adventure for me. I have enjoyed every minute of our collaboration. You and the other thirteen authors of our first book *Student Entrepreneurs: 14 Undergraduate All-Stars Tell Their Stories* have really started something. From the New Orleans launch of book #1, the authors have become "turned on" to book sales. Did it have anything to do with the "party" atmosphere in New Orleans, or the excitement of receiving the first copy of their very own words in print? Perhaps it was because these student-winner dynamos are proven entrepreneurs, and they simply put their minds to work on how to sell, sell, sell yet another product -- this time, their own book.

Dynamic and creative promotional undertakings have occurred. Several authors have posted the book prominently on their companies' web-sites, where customers take advantage of purchasing a copy written by a business colleague. Because our student entrepreneurs have already gained their customers' respect and admiration, these are "easy" sales. Others have planned aggressive email campaigns to spotlight their authorship. One author takes books to each jewelry party and sells them alongside her beau-tiful baubles. Another author's unique sales promotion included prominent displays of the book, greeting each student who walks into the author's campus bookstore.

And now we have book number two, with an entirely new set of student entrepreneurs as authors. This book includes one chapter penned by a student, Ahmad Fouda, from Perth, Australia. He is our first winner from "down under" as Australia and New Zealand just began regional par-ticipation in the awards program in 2003. Welcome to Ahmad and all readers south of the equator.

Just what impact will all these combined authors have on students enrolled on university and college campuses and in high schools? It is really too soon to tell, but avid interest in the first book gives us an insight into what will transpire. Let's take a flight of fantasy into the future -- several years from now. The authors have been active, talking up entrepreneurship in their communities, on radio and TV, in the press, and on their campuses. In high demand, they spread the word of making ethical business decisions and living a student entrepreneur's life with all the rewards it brings. Utterances to be heard include:

"I march to a melody of my own orchestration."

"I can hire and fire myself."

"I balance pop quizzes with payrolls."

"I love life in the 'entrepreneurial fast lane.'"

"I run my business and I am an author."

"I provide employment for others."

"I dance to my own design."

"I give back to enhance my community."

"I am growing my business."

"I make honorable, ethical decisions that are 'good business.'"

"I serve as a role model to other students."

In high school, university, and college classrooms, the book will be incorporated into entrepreneurship, marketing, business, and ethics courses. Since our authors represent disciplines across campus, in each of these disciplines the authors will be held up as representative of what can be accomplished within each major by looking through an entrepreneurial lens. The book will spread entrepreneurship from the walls of the business schools to the halls of liberal arts, education, communication, engineering, architecture, history, etc. The authors will become the superstars they are destined to be. They will challenge sports stars for the spotlight because of the positive impact their businesses have, and will continue to have, on the economy.

The reputation and scope of the Global Student Entrepreneur[SM]

Awards continues to grow. In 2004, China, Sweden, and Spain joined our ranks, and I am currently in discussions with others in Europe for 2005 involvement. Our contest is being translated into numerous languages around the globe -- Spanish, Chinese, Swedish, and French -- in order to be inclusive and encourage youth entrepreneurship.

In the introduction I wrote for the first book, I reflected on the childhood activity of running a lemonade stand, which is often the first entrepreneurial endeavor undertaken by many of our winners. These sticky-hot-summer-day, role-playing adventures are carried out in a collaborative environment, where friends, siblings, and parents are drafted for roles as salesperson, sign painter, clean-up crew, and purchasing agent (isn't it usually Mom who runs off to the store for cups and lemonade?). What a great training ground this cooperative collaboration provides!

The Global Student Entrepreneur[SM] Awards, which produces our authors, has been a collaborative endeavor from the start. Being a very collaborative kind of person myself -- I love teamwork and the resulting energy and creativity flowing from it -- it was a natural to bring in others as the awards were built.

Jeanne Rhodes has kept the administrative end of things humming along at Saint Louis University and is integrally involved in getting out the annual competition announcement. Plus, she is a great energizer and organizer of the students who work in our office at Saint Louis University's John Cook School of Business. Each year, four or five students lend their energy to the chores involved in running the program. And what better focus group could we find than a group of students to run new ideas by and determine what appeals to them and to other students? Since I am long out of undergrad life, I often rely on the ideas and insights of the student generation. Thanks to Jeanne and to all the students who have helped.

Two student collaborators deserve my special commendation.

Robin Rath worked in our office for the entire four years he spent at Saint Louis University, and in the year and a half since graduation, he has set up his own business designing websites. (I hope that the environment in our Jefferson Smurfit Center for Entrepreneurial Studies (JSCES) may have influenced his choice of a career. We believe that entrepreneurship, like the flu, can be contagious.) Thanks to Robin, our new GSEA website, www.gsea.org, has been designed to specifically appeal to college/university students. The site draws on Robin's creative talent to assist us in spreading the GSEA word. Interest and hits to our website continue to grow, and we thank you, Robin, for your part in this growth.

The second student is Jordan Koene, who we snagged as a freshman to work in the Center. Jordan's eternal smile and enthusiasm brighten up our office. Jordan spent a semester in Spain on Saint Louis University's Madrid campus. During that time, he assisted SLU/Madrid to get the awards program up and running throughout Spain. They relied on his knowledge of the program to launch their own awards. We are proud that one of our student teammates was directly responsibility for expansion! Thanks, Jordan.

If you are a professor or teacher who has used the book in your classroom (or are planning to do so in the future) you have Cathy Bishop to thank. And so do I! Cathy, an educator and author, took up my challenge to collaborate and write the accompanying Instruction Manual for the books. These gems are free to you to download from the website, and they give a wealth of ideas and activities to imprint the lessons from the authors. Cathy was hooked the first time she read the stories, and she commented on the wealth of entrepreneurial information and the energy coming from the authors. Thanks for being a part of this team, Cathy.

Jim Fisher, Director of the Emerson Center for Business Ethics at Saint Louis University, has been an extremely valuable collaborator this year, as we embarked on writing the book using an ethics theme. He provided the expert advice and enthusiasm needed as we expanded into this new arena. He inspired the authors with examples of what they should consider in penning their chapter, and he provided Cathy Bishop with insights and advice for the Instruction Manual. Our hats are off to Jim!

And to Leah Kruger, my primary, daily, minute-to-minute collaborator, goes my admiration and appreciation. She is the one who promotes, publicizes, and prizes each winning student. Her enthusiasm for her job has been a remarkable sight. She brings energy and a youthful vantage point to every situation, from writing a press release to planning the awards ceremony. Leah, GSEA wouldn't be where it is today without you!

And to all our judges, well-wishers, and sponsors I say thanks. Without the hard work of the judges we would have no winners; without well-wishers, we would have no cheering gallery; and without the financial support of the sponsors, there would be no program or prizes. So I salute the GSEA sponsors: The Coleman Foundation, the Kauffman Foundation, Edward Jones, Northwestern Mutual Financial Network, and Enterprise Rent-a-Car. And I thank our 2003 global judges: Rafael Alcaraz, Stedman Graham, Dan Lauer, and Ron Rubin.

If your eyes are on these words, and you have read everything up to this point, I congratulate you. You, like me, are interested in uncovering more about the origins, history, background, and intentions of the book you are reading. I applaud your interest in these student entrepreneurs and the extent to which ethical decisions have come in to play in their businesses. If, when you have read the final page of the book, you want to comment on what you have read, please email us at jsces@slu.edu. We would be most interested in your reactions.

On behalf of all the authors, I say thank you for buying their book. They are tomorrow's entrepreneurial business leaders, and by your purchase you have endorsed their efforts to bring a solid ethical platform to younger generations around the world. You have made your valuable contribution and are to be commended as a collaborator in the effort to promote youth entrepreneurship.

-- Sharon K. Bower

Sharon K. Bower is creator and director of the
Global Student Entrepreneur[SM] Awards and associate
director of the Jefferson Smurfit Center for Entrepreneurial Studies
at the John Cook School of Business, Saint Louis University.

E2-Profiles in Entrepreneurial Ethics

Case studies are invaluable tools for teaching and learning about business. The best cases are true -- actual stories drawn from real businesses in which employees, managers, and owners must make decisions under pressures of time, money, and incomplete information. Students of business who study these cases are challenged to imagine what it would be like to face these real-life decisions, to size up the situation, to select a course of action, and ultimately to explain or even justify their choices.

Stories of entrepreneurship seldom need embellishment. All the elements of high drama are present: bold creativity straining against harsh realities, real rewards sought in the face of daunting risk, and opportunity transformed by the marketplace into value and wealth. These tales embody our aspirations, earn our admiration, and, in many respects, tap an important vein of the "American dream."

But let us temper this optimistic and inspirational view of entrepreneurship with a small note of caution. Entrepreneurs are often testing the boundaries of what is possible, pushing the so-called envelope. Typically, starting a business can make enormous demands on time, energy, and financial resources and may, in the process, strain our ability to meet other important responsibilities.

Young entrepreneurs in particular may lack business experience and thus may not be sure what legal and regulatory requirements apply to their operations. They may not be aware of customary business practices. On the one hand, this may allow them to see new and better ways to do things, but on the other hand, it can lead to mistakes that a more seasoned practitioner might avoid. We learn from our mistakes, but when our errors involve issues of law and ethics, the cost of such missteps can be substantial and painful to ourselves and others.

Finally, successful entrepreneurs, young and old alike, must have confidence in themselves, in their ideas, and in their ability to deliver the goods. But the road to success is seldom short and direct; dead-ends and detours are part of the journey, and what we learn from these challenges can contribute mightily to more positive results and achievements.

We have asked our young entrepreneurs to write a bit about their bumps in the road. More specifically, we asked about the ethical and moral challenges they encountered in the midst of their entrepreneurial activities. We primed the pump with questions such as these:

- How did you balance your other responsibilities as student, family member, or friend with that of entrepreneur?
- Did your business find compliance with laws, codes, or regulations a challenge?
- What about truth-telling? Were you tempted to use "bluffing" tactics in negotiations or to make optimistic promises about performance and capabilities?
- What about raising money, supervising employees, and responding to complaints? How did you know what the right thing to do was? Did you ever find pressures conspiring to prevent you from doing the right thing?

The stories of our Global Student Entrepreneur[SM] Award winners did not disappoint. What they reveal is not the darker side of entrepreneurship, but instead they demonstrate that imagination, hard work, and integrity are at the heart of the entrepreneurial dream. These case studies are profiles of great competence, confidence, and courage.

-- James E. Fisher, Ph.D.
Director, Emerson Center for Business Ethics
Saint Louis University

Chapter One

On the Wings of the Past

Presented by Adam Makos

I will be the first to admit that in my 23 years, I have

been pretty lucky. From a worldly view, I am one in a billion, not in the ego-bound egotistical sense, but rather I am lucky in that for the past 10 years, since the eighth grade, I have worked for myself. My company, *Ghost Wings Magazine*, is a quarterly published military aviation magazine dedicated to "Honoring the Sacrifices of America's Veterans." With a young, talented staff of four (more about them later), I work to preserve and present the stories of America's military defenders, who are the heroes and role models we need today.

Ghost Wings runs my life because I let it. I honestly love my work. How many people can say that? How many of the world's billions love their work, much less love their work as they work for themselves? That is not to say that entrepreneurship is the blissful path to utopia. From the lowly pulpit of one still fresh in the journey, I can attest that business ownership is gut-wrenching, heart-pounding, mind-numbing, and head-aching. Who knows, maybe ten years from now, once I have felt the symptoms, I'll add back-cracking, cataract-spawning, and ulcer-inducing. Perhaps most humbling, troubling, and yet empowering is the cold, hard fact that entrepreneurship, or self-business ownership, entails the power to steer, pull, and manipulate the marionette strings of others' lives. With such responsibility comes the unavoidable burden of ethical decision-making, which, in my opinion, represents the true bottom line.

For 10 years, I have sought to serve those in uniform who have served me, you, and the American way of life. Aside from my endless quest to become a scrupulous editor and an astute businessman, I also wear an author's hat, writing about soldiers, sailors, airmen, and Marines.

From World War II to Vietnam, from Midway to Mogadishu, I have had the opportunity to discover the past from those who were there, and then to regurgitate it, for presentation and preservation's sake. Recounting the history and heritage of hometown heroes is better than fiction any day. Moreover, I write about my peers from prior pasts, like the paratroopers who jumped in darkness on D-Day, 1944, the invasion for Europe's liberation:

> At 8:30 p.m. on June 5, under an overcast sky, the 139 men of Easy Company, 506th Parachute Infantry Regiment, 101st Airborne, left their encampment at Upottery airfield and headed for the C-47 aircraft that would carry them to France. Now coined the "Band of Brothers," they marched in orderly columns, with weapons slung over their shoulders and the pockets of their tan uniforms bulging with ammunition, food, and essential equipment, like hand grenades. They wore their trademarked russet brown leather boots.
>
> The paratroopers of Easy Company had darkened their faces. Their helmets had netting with interwoven pieces of beige canvas. On the sides were spade symbols, stenciled in white. The troopers resembled medieval knights with bulbous armor. Like knights, whose armor had weighed around 100 pounds, they, too, would enter battle beneath 100 pounds of gear. Unlike medieval knights, however, paratroopers did not join their profession by birthright; they were volunteers from all walks of American life, ranging from textile mill workers to Ivy League students. Toughened by the Depression, twenty-two months of arduous training had only added to their potential.

Like me, the young men of whom I write were typically in their early twenties and late teens when they were called to save the world for democracy or to save the world period. From these men, especially Major Richard D. Winters, I have gained insight into the ethics of battlefield leadership, which, surprisingly, bears resemblance to the fundamental blocks of business ethics.

Winters is deservingly among the world's most famous veterans. In the arena of popular culture, he and his men, the paratroopers of Easy Company, were profiled in the HBO mini-series "Band of Brothers," based on the million-copy best selling book, **Band of Brothers**, by Stephen Ambrose. In **Band of Brothers**, Easy Company trooper Robert Rader said that Winters had "turned our lives around. He was openly friendly, genuinely interested in us and our physical training. He was almost shy; he wouldn't say 'sh-t' if he stepped in it." Rader added, "You liked him (Winters) so much you just hated to let him down." Winters has always been described as an "inspirational leader" who believed in himself, his men, and in the Allied cause. The label "citizen soldier" fits him; he had few intentions of making a career out of the military and did not desire medals, glory, or commendations. He sought simply to do his best.

Like me, Winters is from Pennsylvania, and thanks to our proximity, I have had the chance to glean from him some insight into ethical leadership. Winters told me, "Leadership, I think, is an inner strength. You must be able to make up your own mind, (to) think for yourself --what is right and what is wrong? Not only being able to think for yourself and getting out there and being in the front ... but to be fair ... at every step of the way with people you deal with." Fairness, I have found, is an essential ethical consideration that should be applied to a company's internal and external operations. In my experience with **Ghost Wings**, I have discovered the overriding importance of fairness in pricing, for example, in that we price each issue uniformly, across geographic regions and market segments. Therefore, our customers have equal access to **Ghost Wings** at a consistent price. Across our operation, ethical treatment of others comes first and foremost. While profit, growth, and ascension of the industry ladder are goals

of almost every business, with **Ghost Wings** our staff members con-
cur: how we make it is more important than if or when we make it.

We have received a number of humbling accreditations for our work
on **Ghost Wings**, one of which came from Major Winters, who told
me that our staff is "a Band of Brothers." He had noted during our
visits to his home that we worked well as a team as we interviewed
him and scanned his photographs and documentation. Moreover, he
intuitively knew that a five-person magazine cannot take off unless
each wingman holds position in the overriding formation. Winters
told me, "Say, if you fellows stick together, no question, something
good is gonna happen. But you have to be fair to each other to maintain that bond."

For our five person staff at **Ghost Wings**, our bond, our fellowship,
began in 1994. My brother Bryan, friend Joe, and I were in middle
school; Joe and I in eighth grade and Bryan in fifth grade. My sisters
Erica and Elizabeth would join our ranks in the coming years. When
Joe, Bryan, and I began **Ghost Wings** as a newsletter, printed on an
inkjet printer and circulated to family and friends, the "Greatest
Generation" had not yet been named, and "Saving Private Ryan" had
yet to reach the drawing boards. The proposed World War II Memorial
lacked a home and funding. Simply put, interest in the history and
participants of World War II, and more so, the Korean War and
Vietnam War, seemed distant in our nation's conscience. Our modest
newsletter was an answer to such apparent apathy, especially among
our own generation that had little exposure to such history in school.

As our business developed, we came to focus on the human-interest element found in the personal stories of aviation veterans, paratroopers, and support personnel -- basically anyone with a military flight connection and a good story to tell.

In 1999, our staff took an entrepreneurial leap of faith and released our first issue of *Ghost Wings Magazine*, the logical evolution of our newsletter. Our first edition, with 28 pages (four with color), was a far cry from more recent issues that are at least 56 color pages long. During speaking engagements, I am often asked how we funded our first issue of the magazine. Anyone who had seen our ink-jet printed, staple-bound copies of the newsletter would have known that production costs were not an issue. The magazine was a whole new ballgame. Usually the question is rhetorical; the person asking has already read how we funded *Ghost Wings* and desires to hear the story for himself or herself first-hand. And rightfully so, as I typically leave out the story of the car I traded for the magazine.

If I had a nickel for each time I have been asked if I have a rich relative who funds our magazine, I would not need a rich relative even if such a benefactor existed. Others assumed that my parents are or were advertising agency executives or Wall Street financial gurus. When we started *Ghost Wings Magazine*, my father was a counselor and my mother was a homemaker. I was a senior in high school with some money saved up from a multitude of summer jobs. It was time, I felt, to buy my first car: a used one, no doubt-a piece of junk, perhaps. Nonetheless, I thought, it would beat riding in the not-so-magical school bus. Then, the printing quote for the first issue arrived in the mail and with it the question: is it the car or the magazine that is to be or not to be? I chose to throw my lot in with the magazine and to relegate my car dreams to remaining, well, dreams. I recognized that if the magazine lasted for even one issue and paid tribute to only the handful of veterans whose stories lined its scant 28 pages, then it would have been a success. Then and now, I have followed the mantra of "Service above Self," often chimed by Senator John McCain, a naval aviator and POW during the Vietnam War.

Ghost Wings survived its first issue, and in the blink of an eye we had produced issues 10 and 11. Our progress, however, was not necessarily smooth sailing. With the release of the first issue we discovered that *Ghost Wings* was seen as "counter-culture" in small academic circles. While our magazine debuted in the late 1990s to great fanfare and among a surge of World War II popular interest, there were several high schools that refused to allow *Ghost Wings* onto their library bookshelves because the magazine concerned the military. Yet, following September 11, 2001, when America's eyes turned to her fighting forces, the message of *Ghost Wings* appeared to mesh with the times.

Nevertheless, anti-military sentiment still remains an issue. In the not so distant past, Vietnam veterans were chastised in numerous ways, including the infamous "baby killer" invective of the 1960s. However, I can think of few examples more insidious than the need for an American university to post a non-discrimination waiver on its application, promising veterans equal treatment. For example, when I recently requested information from a particular graduate school, the application's fine print revealed one answer: the university "does not discriminate against any person because of age, ancestry, color … or veteran status." Another application was more specific in printing

"Vietnam veteran status." No doubt there have been past wrongs against our men and women of uniform in the halls of higher learning. The waiver itself is incriminating.

Before we had even started ***Ghost Wings Magazine***, we confronted an ethical question that would define the core product of our business and its present and future paths. During the summer of 1998, we attended the "Wings of Eagles" air show at the National Warplane Museum in upstate New York. Our goal was to collect material for our first issue of the magazine. There, a handful of protesters marched outside the event's gates with signs that read "War Planes Make War." They were right; some aircraft are used in war. However, their signs could have also read that "War Planes End Wars," and "War Planes Defend Peace." While the protesters illuminated a potential objection to our work, we had long before decided that we would not publish stories that glorify war. Such stories would have been the last things desired by our veteran contributors, friends, and readers. That potential dilemma was easy to identify and resolve. We have yet to meet a veteran who would not agree whole-heartedly with our stance that war is hell yet still sometimes necessary. The war fighter knows better than anyone that armed conflict is an often unavoidable scourge of humanity. "How did they do it?" is the age-old question that historians ask of those who have fought for their country, enduring life's least redeeming pursuit with courage and often nobility. The search for that answer reveals a lesson in humanity that has incredible value now and for our future.

In publishing the stories of military veterans, we have come to understand that our nation can lessen the risk of future war by knowing how to first recognize and then confront a gathering threat. Conversely, the best way for a nation to generate new wars is to forget the old ones, ignoring the dynamics that spark conflict or to look entirely to the future. History often does repeat itself, like it or not, because people do not take time to study the successes, failures, and most importantly, the lessons of the past.

The suffering and conflict that results from the disregard of history is not our nation's only shortcoming. Equally negligent is our propensity to overlook the individuals in the military whose blood, sweat, and tears have forged our present freedom and prosperity. *Ghost Wings* is determined to reverse that trend because we realize that "Freedom isn't Free." From the first issue forward, *Ghost Wings* has followed a mission of "Honoring the Sacrifices of America's Veterans." We print this phrase on our cover and focus on publishing the true, human-interest stories of American service personnel of the 20th century onward. We present the accounts of soldiers, sailors, airmen, and Marines in their own words and publish stories of factual history, not the third party editorial commentary that is often culpable for the glorification of war. Those service personnel who have "been there" are the last to make such a mistake.

Believe it or not, *Ghost Wings*' past, present, and likely future can be charted and predicted at this moment, for we intend to stay true to our mission. Our values remain rooted in the words of an inscription on a battlefield monument in Europe:

To the dead, the honor.
To the living, the lesson.

Chapter Two

Being the Role Model

Presented by Ahmad Fouda

Being an entrepreneur comes with many challenging tasks. However, as an entrepreneur, you also become a role model; therefore, you have to improve your attitude and morality. More importantly, it is the ethics that you practice that determine whether you will have a positive or negative impact on others.

By starting Rook's Events with my long time friend Aziz Dardah, I had to physically and mentally change myself because people started to look up to me, wanting advice and help in starting their own enterprises. Rook's Events is centered on running basketball competitions, such as 3-on-3 games, full-court season games, three-point shoot-out competitions, slam-dunk competitions, and school vocational programs.

During the mid 1990s, basketball was at its peak all over the world. Michael Jordan was winning championships and breaking records. Accessibility to basketball courts and equipment was in strong demand, and TV ratings were starting to beat other traditional sporting events all over the world. Unfortunately, not all good things stay strong, and the popularity of basketball started to dip. It became so bad here in Australia that they pulled all NBL (National Basketball League) games off TV.

Basketball in Australia was starting to struggle, and the big companies that ran 3-on-3 basketball competitions closed or went bankrupt. The 3-on-3 basketball competitions were my favorite as players didn't need a full squad to play, and it was fast and exciting. During mid-2002, there were no 3-on-3 basketball competitions held at all in Perth, Western Australia.

It was about this time that I came up of the idea of creating a business that would run basketball competitions. Having competed in past competitions, we would have the advantage of knowing how to run the games and the real problems involved. There was still just one problem: I did not know anything about starting or running a business, and the degree I was studying was a non-business major. However, this did not stop me from going out there and finding as much information about entrepreneurship as I could. To my amazement, I discovered many organizations and resources that assist and guide young people in starting and running their own business. It was as if I had entered an uncharted continent of Earth. The amount of information available is so vast that to think starting a business is impossible or for the rich is ridiculous.

At first, there were only two people, Aziz and I, who were outpacing each other to try to organize everything. For example, I was organizing the marketing, budget, management, and administration, while Aziz was securing funds by posting flyers and approaching basketball venues to try to get teams to sign up and pay to compete in the initial 3on3 basketball competition, which would have over a $1000 worth of prizes. It was around this time we made our first mistake. The mistake was doing too many jobs at once. Sure, we entrepreneurs think we are superheros, but boundaries must be drawn in order to succeed in a business. We learned that you must delegate big tasks to other people according to their skills and not overtax yourself or any other person with too many jobs.

At this stage, I came up with five different job titles for our staff:
Manager: Responsible decision maker who can lead and plan.

Salesperson: Understands the people within communities -- in our case, basketball culture and community -- and also knows how to talk to them and win their confidence.

Worker: Every business needs workers because you cannot do all the work yourself. Having workers for business start-ups is very difficult, and in Rook's case, we only had volunteers in the beginning.

Administrator: Keeps accounts and organizes paperwork.

Entrepreneur: The problem solver who continually wants to succeed by taking calculated risks.

As we started to take shape and attract interest, we realized that so many more tasks needed to be completed in order to make our first competition a success. Our first competition had to be a success so that following competitions would also succeed. To turn Rook's 3on3 concept into a success, we knew that marketing the competition would be the difference between success and failure. The first thing we had to do was to decide on a stadium for the competition. Out of four major stadiums in Perth, we chose Wally Hagan Stadium in Hamilton Hill because it

· is one of the highest attended basketball arenas in Perth;

· has four basketball courts that can cater eight simultaneous games;

· hosts state basketball teams and is an official state basketball arena;

· is a state basketball arena, therefore making easier to market the competition to more people around the city.

Because we target the youth of Perth (between the ages of 16 - 24), we are continually approaching sponsors who are also targeting the same age group. To make the competition successful, Rook's needed young people to know about the competition, and what better way than radio? We approached Groove 101.7 FM radio station, which is run "by the youth for the benefit of the youth." Not only did we get them to broadcast our competition, but they also became a major sponsor of the competition.

After Groove 101.7 FM became a major sponsor, other big sponsors approached us. We had to ponder what type of sponsors would best benefit the youth of Perth. As Rook's is run by youth, we knew that the majority of the youth in Perth enjoy spending their weekends in nightclubs. As most nightclubs in Perth target the youth, it was difficult to choose a nightclub. We finally chose the Marble Bar. The only other major sponsor we were after was the Department of Health. Because Rook's was encouraging physical sporting competitions between youth, the Department of Health was more than happy to become a major sponsor. As the government was having a major youth campaign of drug and alcohol awareness, Rook's approached the Alcohol and Drug Department within the Department of Health to become sponsors, and they also happily agreed.

We were running sports competitions, so we knew our referees had to be on top of their game as the competitors were playing for money (up to $1000). Wally Hagan stadium has a state basketball team, so it was clear that the stadium had well qualified referees. However, there was still some concern over referee bias, so Rook's 3on3 hired external officiators to make the referees' decisions easier and so that all complaints could be addressed fairly.

At last, the big day arrived. The way we organized, performed, and reacted would be viewed by hundreds, and all personnel involved were nervous, especially me. This was the biggest test in Rook's short but exciting history. All was on the line, but as an entrepreneur, I was always quietly confident. Thankfully, the event was a success, but we were still overworked. The only solution was to get more workers or volunteers. This became no problem as other organizations grew interested in helping us run these competitions. Sadly, we had to turn down many of them, as their main aim was profit maximization. But this does not mean that the word profit is a dirty word. In contrast, profit is a necessity for a business to operate and grow, and that is what every entrepreneur should be aiming for, provided that the community benefits from your efforts.

As Rook's has progressed, we have realized that we can not only benefit the players with just a competition to win, but we can in turn such a competition into a regular community event. We also realized that we can send a powerful message to the youth to help them with their problems. For example, in the neighborhood where most of our competitions are held, Hamilton Hill, drug use is a major problem. Therefore, we worked in conjunction with Wally Hagan stadium to support the Department of Drug and Alcohol awareness campaign. Rook's is proud to say that we are the only youth-based business that runs free seminars, teaching youth everything about social entrepreneurships. Everyone that works for Rook's 3on3 has realized that the youth of Australia have great potential in anything, including business ideas. The problem is that young people often do not know how to transform their ideas into real-life business practices.

Currently, we are running seminars on how Rook's started out, focusing on the difficulties. The most important topic we cover is how we can help young individuals or groups into actually starting their own businesses or social enterprises. We did not create these seminars to tell people what to do but instead to build their confidence and capacity to help themselves and their communities. Another important factor we teach is that a social enterprise should focus not only on profit but also on the community needs; nevertheless, profit is still essential for a business to run.

The major reason I do what I do to help others is that I was in their same situation before I started Rook's. When people of the same age group came up to me and asked for advice, and I gave them advice, that's when I realized that I was becoming the role model. It is important for all entrepreneurs to adopt this role in an ethical fashion. To me, being an entrepreneur is the ultimate role model for today's youth, and I cannot underestimate the power it has to influence young people in a positive manner.

Truthfully, I did not realize what an encouraging impact I had on people until one of my lecturers informed me. Being an entrepreneur comes with many surprising rewards. All in all, starting a business is the best thing that has happened to me.

In closing, I want to leave you with some questions to ask yourself before you start your business: What is the aim of my business? What product or service will I sell? Who are my potential customers? Where will I base my business? What equipment will I need? What price will I charge? How will I find my customers? How will I make them buy from me instead of my competitors?

Finally, another important question to consider as a young entrepreneur is "How might I be able to use my business to help my customers and potentially to improve the community?"

Chapter Three

From Good Roots We Grow

Presented by Andy Szatko

I wasn't born an entrepreneur; I didn't grow up

thinking about selling, and I never had the notion of operating my
own company. I was born healthy; I built forts with my friends, and I
loved the severe weather that always rolled across the Midwest in the
springtime. In fact, I'm sure my life was pretty similar to many of
you reading this book. It is for this reason that I want to share with
you and reassure you that anything is possible, even as improbable as
it may seem to you right now.

Ever since I was seven years old, I knew that I wanted to be a mete-
orologist. Ask my family or friends, and they will tell you I was definitely set on it. When I was choosing a college, I was told that students
change majors all the time, and that if I didn't choose a major right
away, it was all right. I was set, though; I knew I was going into
meteorology because I loved the weather. Well, sure enough, during
my first semester at the University of Nebraska at Lincoln (UNL), I
changed my major because my love for the weather wasn't based on
the desire to sit in an office looking at radar screens. I wanted to be
outside, watching and chasing those big thunderstorms each spring. I
think if I had to pinpoint when I truly became an entrepreneur, it was
at this point. Things began to click in my mind and heart. I started
to think back: when I was growing up, my dad, Ron 'Sam' Szatko,
built every piece of furniture and remodeled every room in our home,
built various items for people who asked, and donated items for raffles
and auctions at our church. Then my mind wandered to a job I had
before I began college, working at a nursery and landscape store.
When I was working there, I began to gain a greater appreciation for
the outdoors and the landscaping industry. I do not recall any time
when I did not want to go to work; instead, I looked forward to it

and had fun when I was there.

So there I was, sitting in my room at college, with ideas of actually starting my own company swirling through my head. But would running my own company actually work for me? Many of you can probably relate to this because it can be pretty intimidating trying to start your own company. Why not wait until you are out of school and can make some money and experience to start a company? The reason for me was that it wasn't fun having to wait. I was so excited about these ideas that I wanted to take a crack at it now; I wanted to be my own boss, and most of all I wanted to run my company the way I wanted to. My parents raised me to be honest, hardworking, and to enjoy life; establishing those kinds of roots has been very important to my success.

My first full season of running Grassroots Landscaping went very well. I was keeping busy with referrals from family, friends, and my first clients. Since school started in August and was in Lincoln, Nebraska (I started the company in Omaha, about one hour northeast of Lincoln), I had to stop taking on new clients a few weeks before I left. During the course of the season, I became excited by how successful this company could potentially become, so I decided to go to school at the University of Nebraska at Omaha (UNO) for my sophomore year. By doing this, I was able to spend more time working later into the season, developing the company for the next season, and spending more time with my future wife Melissa.

Staying in Omaha for my sophomore year was probably one of my best choices I've made, considering my largest project would come from it. Because I switched majors my freshman year, I did not start any of my core horticulture classes until I was at UNO. When classes started, my landscape design and plant identification classes were fairly small, and the professor, Steve Rodie, seemed nice. My classmates and I quickly got to know each other because of the large amount of time that the course required in order to do well in it. I found there was another student in my class who ran a landscaping company that built a lot of retaining walls, just as I did. With both of us being familiar with retaining walls and our professor needing some walls built himself, we started talking about the project for his home. We helped Steve with the colors, style of block, and budget of the project and from that, landed the job. Not only was this project the biggest either of us had worked on, but it was highly visible in the neighborhood as Steve is a well-known person in the horticulture community. When we completed the project, it looked great! Steve and his neighbors gave a thumbs-up to the project, and I now had a great portfolio builder and contact into the horticulture industry.

The time I spent in Omaha flew by, and before I knew it, I was back in Lincoln taking classes. I was very fortunate financially because I had saved enough money working, and my parents would send extra money to support me so that I did not have to get a job while in school. I was determined to get out of school in four years, so I took 18 credit hours a semester to accomplish that. School by far was the most important thing I had to concentrate on, not just because my family wanted me to, but because I wanted to be knowledgeable and set myself apart from others in the landscaping industry. This meant that I had to turn some clients down because it would interfere with my studies. It was hard at times to choose school over the company, but I knew in the end it would benefit me greatly. During these two years in Lincoln, I was constantly working on the company in my spare time, and every weekend I would drive up to Omaha to work and see my fiancée and family. It was pretty hectic sometimes, especially in the spring, when I would drive up to Omaha right after classes to work on projects.

Having that pressure of schoolwork and quality work for my clients, I would sometimes contemplate how I could cut a corner here or not do an assignment there. For example, a retaining wall I was building required me to excavate a substantial amount of soil in order to get the proper amount of gravel backfill behind the wall so that water would not build up. In order to do this, I needed to rent a large skid loader. Since I rented the equipment, it needed to be back by a certain time or else I would be charged extra for keeping it too long. I was able to get most of the hill excavated, but there was one spot where I didn't go far enough back. I didn't want to hand dig farther back, so I thought about just leaving it the way it was since the client wouldn't be able to see behind the wall anyway. The more I thought about it, the more I realized that the only benefit from not cutting farther back into the hill would be a couple hours saved. I was there to provide quality work that would last for this client, and if I didn't do what I said I would do, then why did I start this company in the first place? I decided to go back to my roots: to be honest, hardworking, and to enjoy life. I was honest with myself because I knew the wall had to be installed the correct way. I worked very hard to make sure that wall was the best wall because that's what my clients deserve for their money. And I definitely enjoyed working on that wall because I made a great friend in the client for whom I was working.

Remember, opportunities will come to you when you least expect them. One of my good friends, Kiersten, who was also attending UNL, and I met and began talking with someone from the Entrepreneurship Department. While talking, she mentioned me and how I had been running my business while in school. That caught his attention since he was working with the Northern Great Plains region of the Global Student Entrepreneur Award (GSEA). We got in contact, and he gave me an application to fill out for the award. Lucky for me, I had just finished writing a business plan, had a new brochure put together, and had my website updated. I combined all of it into the application and submitted it. Since I never took any business courses and assumed there would be plenty of others apply-ing for the award, I figured I probably wouldn't win. A few months after I applied, I received an email asking me to RSVP for the awards presentation, which would be in conjunction with the Lincoln Chamber of Commerce after hours. I turned around and said to Melissa, "Well, I didn't win." I went ahead and said the two of us would be attending since it would be a great networking event. When the day came for the presentation, I was working on a retain-ing wall in Lincoln and commuting to Omaha almost every day because I found a house and was starting to move back to Omaha since graduation was coming fast. On my days off from school, I would commute from Omaha to work on this wall, and since I assumed I didn't win the award, I missed the presentation so that I was able to finish the wall and not have to commute anymore. Two weeks later, I was having dinner at my parent's house, and my mom handed me a letter from the mail. I opened it up and started reading. A huge grin appeared on my face, and I immediately read it to my parents. The letter revealed that I had in fact won first place in the

Northern Great Plains region of GSEA. My parents were extremely excited and proud of me. Later, I learned that people were trying to find out where the first place winner was, and that the presentation was a red carpet event. When they announced the winner, they mentioned my name, and that I was probably out working since it was such a nice day out. Little did they know that they were absolutely right.

Things haven't slowed down at all since I graduated in May of 2003. I married my long-time love Melissa, who helps me stay focused and motivated. She is a preschool teacher, and during her summers off, helps run the company during the busiest time of the year. I also have recently joined with my father to offer custom carpentry to my clients. He can build everything from bridges to birdhouses to almost anything that can be made out of wood. New equipment and employees are just a couple of the things that are being added to Grassroots Landscaping, Inc. as we continue to grow.

To be an entrepreneur, you have to have good roots to grow from. When an oak tree first starts to grow, it needs some help and support to get going. As it starts to get some height and strength to it, it starts to sustain itself, finding its own water and food. Then, once big enough, it becomes a place where people use it to tie a swing to, escape the hot summer sun, or figure out where they are. None of that growth will come if that oak tree doesn't have the roots to hold itself up. When entrepreneurs first start out, they need to talk with people, join groups, and figure out what it is going to take to be successful. Then, with a little time, entrepreneurs begin to develop their own place in their industry, adapting and improving the way they do business. Soon, people begin to look at entrepreneurs and see how they are benefiting and supporting others. Just like the oak tree, if entrepreneurs do not have good ethical roots to grow from, it will only take one stiff wind to knock them over.

I have just one more tip for a successful business: thank everyone who has helped you along the way. It is amazing how far a thank-you goes in today's world. So, let me take this opportunity to thank my wife, my parents, my sister, all of my friends, my professors at UNO and UNL who have all supported me, and the GSEA who have given me more than they know.

Chapter Four

E-Business Ethics

Presented by Brian Bushell

The raw size and marketing power of the

Internet has intrigued me since its inception. Through the Internet over the past twenty-four hours, I've played chess with an art student on Via San Zanobi in Florence, Italy; viewed a live weather feed from the top of the Marriott Hotel Aruba, and even learned Spanish from a digital university that exists only in cyberspace. And I've done all this without ever leaving the comfort of my own apartment in Manhattan. If used correctly and ethically, the Internet is unquestionably the most efficient means of marketing, commerce, and information distribution. My personal fascination with the Internet as a business tool has driven me to come up with about three new e-business models every week since I was fifteen years old. This is just something I've always done while in class, at the gym, on the golf course, or wherever else I might be. Sometimes I think the ideas are so great that I jot them down on a napkin, a textbook, or even the back of my hand, so that I might do further research on them when I get to a computer. My research usually discourages me for one reason or another because in the past eight years, I've only launched two of these business models: True University Media and the Memory Foam Factory. True University Media is a marketing company that utilizes a tactic I like to call "Empowerment Marketing," and the Memory Foam Factory, the company I will focus on in this chapter, is an e-retailer of specialty comfort products. This company began as a small venture that targeted college students across North America. But due to the reach and marketing power of the Internet, within two years it has grown to accrue customers in six countries on three continents.

NASA Engineers originally developed Memory Foam for pressure relief during space travel. The material is truly unique because it actually molds itself to the shape of each individual user, providing an amazing combination of support and comfort. The past few years have seen this product's entrance into the bedding industry, and its adoption rate has grown exponentially since 2001. We launched the Memory Foam Factory in May 2002 with the plan that we would only sell the highest quality Memory Foam products to our customers, and would price our products slightly below those of our competitors with the goal of moving a large number of products.

Utilizing this unique material in all of our products, we knew that if our marketing tactics reached a critical mass, our profit margins would be substantial enough to make the venture profitable. The plan was to keep our costs down by targeting college students, executing grassroots marketing tactics, and shipping directly from the factory. Our underlying assumption was that if college students adopted our products, the buzz would spread quickly because college students are extremely vocal, technologically savvy, and confined to small geographic locations.

Essentially, the Internet gives all customers access to their personal Memory Foam Factory kiosk. Therefore, every customer shops from the comfort of his or her own home or office, on his or her own, and sometimes chaotic schedule. Empowered by the Internet when you shop at the Memory Foam Factory, you feel as if you are the only customer on the face of the earth; you will never have to wait in line, and the site speaks directly to you as an individual, no matter how many customers are simultaneously logged onto the company's website.

Despite the marketing and distribution capabilities of this virtual community, when it comes to e-commerce, the Internet is still in its infancy. In 2003, only 8% of all consumer spending in the United States occurred online. This statistic is illogical. The U.S. is the most technologically advanced country in the world, and the Internet is unquestionably the most efficient method of shopping for and purchasing non-perishable goods. After all, e-retailers don't have to pay for physical retail space, so e-commerce pricing structures are often significantly less expensive than those institutions with conventional means of sales and distribution.

If this is the case, then why is such a small percentage of shopping done online? One reason is that, people, especially Americans, are creatures of habit. Five years ago, if you wanted to buy a pair of sneakers, you went to your local sneaker store. If you planned on seeing a movie at 8:00 PM on a Saturday night, you would have been sure to get to the theater early enough to purchase your tickets and get good seats. Today there is a more efficient solution to these and other retail related problems, and yet many people still insist on using conventional distribution methods to purchase products and services. Consumers don't use e-commerce to its fullest potential because, as a group, they are afraid of sacrificing privacy and security for products that they can't physically touch prior to purchase and that are marginally less expensive than those that can be purchased at conventional retail locations. E-retailers and entrepreneurs must do their part to dispel this fear and help e-commerce reach its maximum potential. To accomplish this, e-retailers must ensure that each customer's shopping experience is honest, straightforward, and pleasurable. The only way to ensure this is for all e-retailers to abide by a self-imposed code of business ethics. Above all, these companies must always represent themselves, their policies, and their products honestly and accurately.

Think about ethics as it applies to your daily life. As a student, you are faced with ethical situations every day. How you deal with and react to these situations is a direct reflection on you, your character, and therefore, your reputation. If you never go to class, your professors will think you don't care. If you constantly cheat on your significant other, people will question your honesty. As e-entrepreneurs and business people, we face slightly different situations. However, just as in the social world, our actions in the professional world can build or break our reputations, and our reputations can be our most valuable non-quantitative assets. Conversely, they can be our biggest nemesis.

In the world of e-business, one's reputation is extremely crucial because information on the Internet is relatively unobstructed and free flowing. If we perform some type of shady activity, it will be recognized in a short period of time. Therefore, as a member of this mammoth virtual community, all users are expected to represent themselves in an accurate and ethical manner. Any company that misrepresents itself online is not only doing its industry a disservice, but is also directly hindering the adoption rate of e-commerce among Internet users worldwide. Ask yourself the following question: Am I more likely to tell my friends about a shopping experience that went as I expected it to go, or about a shopping experience that left me feeling as if I'd been violated? I'll venture a guess that you'd feel compelled to vent about the latter. Therefore, each e-commerce transaction that goes awry, for one reason or another, negatively and exponentially affects the adoption rate of e-commerce among Internet users.

When consumers make the decision to shop for and purchase various products online, they are sacrificing the ability to see and touch the respective products before they purchase them. Unfortunately, some e-retailers take advantage of this fact by misrepresenting their products, services, and policies, figuring that the return process for the purchased product will be too great a hassle or expense for the consumer to fol- low through with, and therefore the sale will remain, regardless of the product's quality. This unfortunate statistic is very influential in holding e-commerce back from reaching its maximum potential. As bad as this may seem from a consumer's perspective, for ethical e-retailers competing in industries with slim margins, such unethical activity becomes extremely destructive.

Imagine for a moment that you are in the business of selling gold watches over the Internet. You know that in addition to your site, there are five other companies that sell identical watches, and they buy their watches from the same supplier you do. Since all five com- panies buy the same products from the same supplier, you know that everyone pays the same or similar prices for their inventory. Now imagine that one of those five competitors begins selling its watches online for the same price that you buy them for from your supplier. What might you suspect is going on? Might you suspect that your competitor is being dishonest in some way? My guess is that you would suspect that your competitor has switched to selling gold plated watches instead of solid gold watches but has not changed its relative advertising and marketing campaigns accordingly. How do you think this situation might affect your company's sales? How would you react to and deal with this situation? This is the situation I found myself in not long ago.

In February 2002, I noticed that one of my competitors had reduced its pricing structure to a point that would be unattainable for our company to reach as long as we continued to sell our high quality product line. Therefore, I suspected that this competitor was actually selling a product inferior to the one displayed on its website and therefore drastically misrepresenting itself, deceiving its customers, and breaking the law. I knew that if this was in fact the case, the Memory Foam Factory could not compete with this company and remain ethical. In other words, we couldn't sell a truly high quality product at the same price that our competitor had priced its products. I also suspected that the company must have a significant number of unhappy customers out there spreading negative "buzz" about the Memory Foam industry.

This is a very destructive scenario because it not only decreases your market share and overall profit, but it lowers overall consumer confidence. Each time a consumer engages in e-commerce, the quality of the received product will often dictate whether or not that consumer will make another online purchase in the future. Not only does this dishonest activity immediately and directly affect your company's sales, but it also negatively affects future sales across many e-commerce industries. This is the situation that I found myself in.

Suspecting that my competitor was engaged in fraud, and therefore unlawfully stealing business away from the Memory Foam Factory, I knew that I had to do something quickly to rectify the situation, or we would continue to lose substantial market share. However, I knew that before I could do anything, I had to prove my theory, and the most efficient way to do that was to order one of my competitor's products and determine the quality of the product by testing its density.

The quality of Memory Foam is generally determined by its density. For example, a four-pound piece of Memory Foam is of higher quality than a three-pound piece with the same dimensions. Similarly, a four-pound piece of this material is also more expensive than a three-pound piece, both at the wholesale and the retail level of distribution. Since few people are versed in the determination of a product's density, most consumers simply accept the retailer's stated product specifications to be true, and therefore never perform their own quality evaluations. Memory Foam is also a fairly "new to the world" product. This "newness" results in a consumer that, frankly, doesn't know what to expect when the product arrives at his or her doorstep. This fact adds another level of confusion into the mix, making the inferior product even less likely to be detected.

When the competitor's product was delivered to me, I tested its density three times, and as I suspected, it was an inferior product and not the one represented on the e-retailer's website. Specifically, the product that the company advertised to have a density of four pounds per cubic foot in reality had a density of about 2.8 pounds per cubic foot. This discrepancy is unacceptable by any scientific means of standard deviation.

In such a situation, the first thing you must do is determine your ultimate goal of any chosen course of action. In this case, my goal was to get this competitor to remove permanently all false product density claims on its website. After you determine your goal, the next thing to do is list all potential courses of action. The first and most obvious course of action is to call your competitor, state your business and your findings, and demand a refund and a change in the company's advertising policy, or you will report the organization to the Better Business Bureau. The second alternative is that you make these demands, but make them in the form of a notarized or legal type letter. The third is that you execute either one of the two prior alternatives but do so anonymously. And the fourth alternative is that you skip contacting the organization altogether and go right to a regulatory agency like the Better Business Bureau with your findings.

If you choose to identify yourself to your competitor, you will immediately draw unwanted attention to your company. Essentially, you will turn this competitor into an enemy and make an already competitive industry increasingly cutthroat. However, if you do not identify yourself, you run the risk that this competitor will not take your threat seriously enough to rectify the situation. If you skip notifying the company altogether and go directly to a regulatory agency, it is very unlikely that anything at all will be done to rectify this situation.

I chose to rectify the situation through an anonymous and legal type letter. In my letter, I identified myself as a customer, which I was since I had purchased the competitor's product. I claimed that I had chosen to remain anonymous so that the company would rectify its faulty claim with all of its customers. Moreover, it was the only way I could be sure that I wouldn't be given any precedence over any other customers. I also demanded that the company rectify all faulty advertising claims within a given period of time. If all of my demands were not met, I'd be forced to take legal action.

The method proved to be successful because my requests were fulfilled, and therefore, my goal was achieved. Since the letter succeeded in motivating the recipient to rectify its faulty advertising campaign, I effectively and temporarily increased the "honesty level" within the online memory foam industry. I maintain that in any industry, the only attribute that customers and retailers can demand of one another is honesty. Without honesty, consumers will lose confidence, advertising costs will increase because it will take a lot more "convincing" to convert each sale, and the efficiency of our consumer-driven economy will become jeopardized.

In e-business, or in any business where there is some semblance of anonymity, it is extremely important to carry out all transactions and activities ethically. Without certain self-imposed business ethics, consumer confidence will decrease, online prices will increase when e-retailers make their modest attempt to compensate for the decrease in volume, and e-commerce will never grow to its maximum potential. Therefore, without business ethics, we as consumers and entrepreneurs will be without our most efficient means of marketing, commerce, and information distribution available to date: the Internet.

Chapter Five

Determined to Be "A Cut Above the Rest"

Presented by Chiquita Miller-Nolan

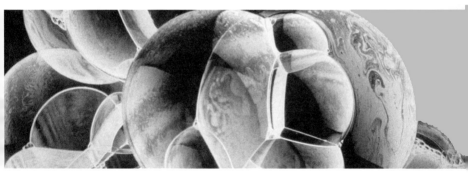

The biggest challenge of being an entrepreneur is the process. When I opened my business, Royal Touch Salon Plus, I had been a stylist for ten years. I worked in the Houston/Humble, Texas area for about two years before I opened my own salon. The saying, "Necessity is the mother of invention" was true for me as there were two immediate needs I desired to meet.

The first need was more options, such as flexibility and control concerning my career because I was and am a wife and mother. I have three children, and I was feeling guilty about working. Although neither of my girls ever went to daycare unless I worked there, when I had my son, we tried daycare for a brief period. I was never comfortable with leaving him. Therefore, it didn't take many times of his coming home with scratches that the daycare could not explain for me to consider other options.

At the time, I was a stylist for JC Penney. I loved the security the company gave; yet, for the first time, it wasn't enough. My second need was job satisfaction, and Penney's couldn't give me what I needed. One thing that I tell people who are not satisfied with their job is "What you do for someone else, you can do for yourself. Simply learn all of the 'ins and outs,' along with your personal skills and knowledge, then find the need for what you do, and begin to work at fulfilling it." That's just what I did. With much prayer, I began to realize the solution to my problem would also be a solution to another problem: a lack of multi-cultural styling salons in the Humble, Texas area. I was a hairstylist skilled in all hair types, and that was and is something that's rare for this area. Also, I noticed that many salons had signs saying "No children allowed unless being serviced." The ones that didn't have the signs also didn't have any provisions to occupy children in order to keep them from being a nuisance. In addition, the salons in this area were specialty salons or they catered mostly to one race.

My goal then became to open a full service salon that could treat all hair types, men, women, children, Black, White, Asian, Hispanic, Indian, etc. The next thing I planned to do was to have a play area so mothers like me could bring their children with them. The play area was in a section of the salon where the parents could see their children at the same time they were waiting or being served. The play area included coloring books, reading books, a TV/VCR, children's movies, LEGO blocks, dolls, and other toys. This really helped set us apart from other salons, not to mention that my children could now go to work with me. The clients enjoyed this new "family atmosphere." Even the clients who didn't have children would comment on how well the children would behave because "they had something to do." I was sensitive to the needs of others, so for my clients who were elderly or desired a more relaxed setting, I simply scheduled them when we were the least busy.

In the beginning as I prayed about this whole idea, I saw another benefit that set us apart. We would have a Christian atmosphere. This meant we would not have any loud, annoying music, gossiping, or foul language. Instead, our atmosphere would be edifying. Therefore, our name comes from the scripture *I Peter 2:9*, "you are a Royal Priesthood . . ." thus Royal Touch Salon. The reason we have "Plus" at the end of our name is that we are more than just a salon. I am a minister; therefore, it carries over in everything that I do and touch. I don't have to preach to everyone; I simply live a Christian life before them. When they have problems and need advice I let them talk. When asked, I speak only what I know will be received, and the rest of the time, I just listen and pray.

I keep my business innovative by looking to offer what other salons do not and also by growing with the needs of the business. For instance, I noticed that the salons in my area only treat the client as someone who receives a service, pays for it, and hopefully will come again. However, in keeping true to our name, we must make each client feel like royalty. We do this in both small and big ways.

On Mother's Day, Valentine's Day, Easter, and other special days, we set out breakfast croissants, doughnuts, and juice to show our appreciation. Even if it's not a holiday but an extremely busy day, and the wait may be long, we order food to keep the clients happy. There have been days when we hit a busy time in the evenings, and because the wait was so long, we ordered pizza. No one walked out, and the customers appreciated the concern and felt like they were a part of a family, not just another dollar to be made. I also observed how once the clients felt like this, they developed a loyalty to the business. They referred others and would tell them about the little things we did.

In order to make our income more predictable, I began to observe other salons. I noticed that in Atlanta, many salons offered pre-paid visits, and in our area no one did. My next mission was to come up with a way that this would work for our area. Fortunately, I met a friend on the other side of Houston who made the same observation, and she shared with me how she made it work for her. By incorporating the information she gave me along with what I needed, I customized and instituted The Program.

The Program would once again meet a need on two levels: the clients' and ours. It would meet our need to have a predictable, consistent income, and at the same time meet the clients' need to save money. A regular shampoo, conditioner, and style costs approximately $35. The Program offers four visits for $100 a month, a savings of $40 per month. Payment is due by the first of each month. The Program requires weekly visits, it does not roll over to the next month, and it is limited to the first 20 people who sign up with each stylist. The Program also offers discounts on additional services. It is an attractive offer due to affordability and exclusivity.

Another thing I do is learn from everything and everyone. I may observe something that has nothing to do with a salon, yet I will weigh it out to see how it could be incorporated into the salon. While at a banquet for something else, the idea to have a "Customer Appreciation Event" came to me. We now have it every December, even though what we do for the event may vary. The first year, we held a Customer Appreciation Banquet. During this time, all of our stylists acknowledged their appreciation toward their clients. We each gave certificates of appreciation along with awards. The awards went to the clients with the most referrals in a year, the client who had been with us the longest, and each client that remained on The Program the entire time that year. We also gave out grab bags that held gift certificates and promo materials from other businesses along with lots of door prizes donated from other businesses. We made this event available to every customer and their spouse. The night consisted of entertainment, dinner, and networking. Clients had the chance to introduce their own business to others and network. This was so effective that after the banquet, the clients' husbands became loyal to the salon. Even if they couldn't come themselves, they sent their wives and told them to support us because "We were really doing something."

Since the progress at Royal Touch is perpetual, we have developed a salon newsletter, **The Royal Touch Reader**. This is another way for us to keep in touch with our clients and keep them feeling motivated to be a part of a salon that is "a cut above the rest." The newsletter contains monthly specials, a word from the editor, a beauty tip corner, a feature story, birthday and anniversary announcements along with achievements and advertisements from our clients. It is sent out every two months.

As I said earlier, we change as the business needs change. It has been work to get where we are today. I did not take out a business loan; I simply started with help from my mother-in-law and the favor of God. When I first started, I operated as an Employer/Employee salon. After a year and a half of supplying everything for everyone -- business overhead, advertising, payroll, and employer's tax -- I closed. Although the salon was extremely successful, I was overwhelmed. After I regrouped, I reopened in the same location with a booth rental structure. This was much less stress, and God revealed to me how to do this and yet have the standard that I longed for in a salon.

Since that time, we have moved from a 950 square feet space to our current 1600 square feet facility. We still have not reached my ultimate goal, but we are well on our way. My vision for this location is to employ five stylists, a barber, two nail technicians, a facialist, two receptionists, and expand to a boutique. Once I have this salon over-flowing, then my plans are to branch out and open other salons. I look forward to the day we will have our first franchise and/or investor.

Another need that I sought to fulfill once again was my own. After being a stylist for seventeen years, I have reached the point in my career where I am ready to move from behind the chair to just own-ing and managing. I realized that in order to make the transition, I would need additional training. After praying, God once again revealed to me to take advantage of the opportunities that he has pro-vided. This new quest led me to Kingwood College. I started Kingwood College in the fall of 2002 as a business management major. I will graduate the fall of 2004 with a Small Business Management Certificate. After that, I will finish my degree at my own pace. It was a tremendous challenge to go to school, run a busi-ness, manage a family, and co-pastor a church with my husband, but it has been very rewarding. I realize that as an entrepreneur, there are certain sacrifices that at times must be made in order to achieve the goal that is set. It requires great discipline and the ability to remain focused. A friend of mine often says, "How bad is your 'want-to'?" meaning how bad do you want to do something, and how much are you willing to do to get it? Once you know the answer, then you condition yourself for the sacrifices that lie ahead.

Royal Touch Salon Plus is not just a business but a family. The clients are protective of it, loyal to it, and they appreciate us as much as we appreciate them. We have a mandate: We don't just fix hair, we fix lives. We are located in Atascocita, a suburb of Humble, Texas, a city just northeast of Houston. We are the first black-owned salon of our capacity in the Atascocita area. We are the only salon in this area that does what we do. We are professional, considerate, and sensitive to the needs and desires of our clients.

My advice to anyone with a business idea is to be as realistic as possible concerning it. Study the area being considered to find the need for what you do. Seek to fulfill a need, not just to be a carbon copy of the something that already exists. Once this is done, the business will be sought after, and that is better than being the one doing the seeking. Look at the reality of the situation to make sure that you can fulfill what you say you can, and consider how much knowledge you have concerning your proposed business. Count up the costs and weigh every option to discover the best one. Get feedback from those you survey; don't just count on a paper survey.

Remember, things that look good on paper do not always work out. Talk to people, get the heartbeat of the area you are in, and then meet people where they are. Last but not least, remember -- with God, all things are possible.

Chapter Six

One Step at a Time

Presented by Eric Knopf

For me, chasing a dream always came naturally. I would find myself doodling and daydreaming all day long about inventions and companies I would start someday. It seemed as though every week I had a million dollar idea rolling around in my head. That was when I was eight. When I became old enough to begin to understand what it took to start a business, I found out that my ambition sharply outweighed my abilities. Furthermore, I found that I had what I call the Field of Dreams Syndrome -- "If you build it, they will come." This is when all my ideas occurred in a vacuum, and I assumed everyone in the world wouldn't be able to live without my product if I created it. Soon my adolescent million-dollar business ideas lost their luster as their viability fell short of reality. The biggest bombshell that hit my adolescent and over-zealous entrepreneurial mind was that businesses take work. Furthermore, they demanded answers to difficult ethical questions and situations for which I was not prepared.

When I began high school, I was pursuing a motocross-racing career, and I did not know where it would lead. All I knew was that I was winning races, had some sponsors, and wanted to keep doing it. Besides, it was fun. I came up with hundreds of drawings of shock absorbers, airboxes, hydraulic steering stems, and other equipment I was sure was going to change the industry. I also felt I had a knack for selling people on "stuff" they didn't need or want. It was somewhat of a challenge. Eventually Arlan Lehman, the owner of the company I raced and worked for, gave me a shot at formulating and implementing a marketing plan. He allowed me to put my artistic interest and my consumer knowledge to work doing his company's marketing and advertising. It was a dream job, and I felt I was good at it too! I was working with people I admired and was given a chance. I didn't know it then, but I was the beneficiary of one of the most valuable experiences of my life -- of having a full-time mentor in my life, pushing me and challenging me. I made many mistakes and bad choices, but he was there to correct me and guide me through the mishaps. He taught me more in one summer than any-thing I had ever read or done before. This was the first and most important element of entrepreneurship: Find a mentor who will invest time in you.

Because of my mentor, my sense of identity grew clearer. By the end of high school, I had developed a strong sense of direction in my life, and I had found a new strength through salvation by faith in Jesus Christ. But my life took a drastic change when my motocross-racing friend was paralyzed. Suddenly, my entrepreneurial motor kicked into high gear. My mission was to create my own company that would spread the gospel in new ways that would powerfully influence my generation, such as my friend. This was the second element of entrepreneurship that I have found to be essential: Become passionate about your dreams and visions.

Within a few months after enrolling at Westmont College, I started my first company called The Flood. It was actually a non-profit organization that I started with a few friends. We put on a huge event filled with music, testimonies, and renowned speakers. Over 600 people filled the public park and the event proved an incredible suc-cess. But I found it to be incredibly terrifying as the thought of failure would riddle my mind. I had spent my savings as well as borrowed money from my parents to make it happen at the risk of losing it all.

Thankfully we ended up breaking even, but I found that if I let the thought of failure keep me back, I would never achieve anything. This was the third lesson I learned: Fear of failure will keep you from accomplishing your dreams.

The Flood was only the start because I wanted to do something unique in evangelism. So, I once again started dreaming of my second endeavor. In December 2001, a concept called Epic Life was born. We created and sold clothing, sponsored extreme sports teams and music bands, put on events, and created some of the most cutting-edge marketing and advertising material. We found how important it was to think outside the box. But because Epic Life was socially driven with an evangelistic mission, we suddenly had to address many issues that we hadn't planned on.

My friends and I created clothing out of my dorm room and sold it around the campus. Business was going great and money was coming in, but I found myself examining many ethical issues surrounding my new "business." I had great ambition and passion for Epic Life, but it legally didn't exist, and I was making money illegally. At that time I refused to accept the responsibilities of accounting and the work it would take to follow through to make things sound. It's amazing how when things are going well, it is so much easier to ignore the little formalities and nagging issues. It's almost as if you believe that as small as you are, you are above the legalities, requirements, and responsibilities of starting a business. I found myself with my ambition to be an entrepreneur outweighing my commitment to actually following through with the state and federal requirements. Being young, I didn't understand all the formalities I had to adhere to, and I found myself in trouble when I had to report income and pay my taxes for the year. Until then, I hadn't kept track of invoices and expenses because I didn't know the requirements AND the benefits and tax advantages to good recordkeeping. It took this near encounter with the IRS for me to realize the importance of following through with business requirements and legal formalities.

In the beginning, Epic Life needed an extra push. I felt that I had the vision of what it would take but needed some direction and encouragement. I needed to feel that I was not the only person on board, that others believed in my visions and dreams to create something totally new that would change lives. I dreamed of talking with the three-time motocross champion Greg Albertyn about Epic Life and its mission to reach today's generation. With the combination of my drive, passion, and determination, I somehow found myself three months later in Laguna, California, sitting across from Greg Albertyn. We talked for a couple hours, and I am sure my enthusiasm was nauseating. But something funny happened. He believed in me because he saw how genuinely passionate I was about Epic Life and how much I wanted it. Two months later, I had a near-stranger-turned-mentor named Ted Seitz purchase a several thousand dollar enclosed trailer for Epic Life's motocross machines because he believed in me. He was a very successful businessman in telecommunications and offered incredible advice and direction. But it was his confidence and encouragement that fueled me more than anything. He saw the fire in my eyes and knew that I would push Epic Life all the way. From these two experiences, I learned If you don't set high goals and believe in yourself, no one else will.

Epic Life was starting to roll. We had a brand new trailer, had expanded our extreme sports teams to over twenty members, had a new partner named Austin, and were making lots of clothes. We eventually formed a ministry partnership with Campus Crusade for Christ and began creating our own social movement. Things were great! But as things were growing, I had to deal with a whole new set of ethical issues pertaining specifically to me. Suddenly I was in a very difficult position regarding the integrity of Epic Life and myself. I had to deal with people on our surf team getting involved with alcohol and with seeing our company stickers on street signs, lamp posts, toilet seats, and public buildings. We were supposed to be ambassadors for Christ and be a witness to our peers for a purpose. We also had to be accountable for whom we associated with and how we conveyed our message. I learned several hard lessons about being careful with whom you associate.

During some of these difficult times when our mission was at odds with our actions, I felt it was necessary to seek the council of mentors in my life. I wanted to know that I wasn't making rash decisions based on emotions or my own self interests. So I sought answers to my plaguing questions. Ultimately, I had to decide to let some people go and sever some partnerships because it would ultimately affect Epic Life's mission. Although some individuals did continue to try to block Epic Life's mission, I learned from my mistakes and quickly found that nothing is ever worth compromising your integrity.

I also discovered that most of my obstacles developed from trying to do too much at once. Because it was my dream, my vision, and my company, I thought the best way to manage Epic Life would be to make sure everything was done right by doing it myself! I messed up by trying to be the surf team manager, clothing director, ministry coordinator, and event planner. It was during these times that my incompetence led to my overlooking several ethical issues that I should have been on top of. As soon as I stopped choking Epic Life and started letting other people make a difference, we experienced growth and momentum. We still were (and are) making mistakes, but the difference is that we are much more efficient as a business operation. The lesson is to do only what you are absolutely best at and let others do what they do best. Today, I have passed most of Operations off to Austin who has been able to propel Epic Life in a new direction. It's hard to let go other people take some control, but I had to in order to see Epic Life's vision reach its true potential. In addition, I wanted to know that I helped start something that would-n't die if I left.

Another problem that I still encounter is that I always want to grow too fast. I focus too much on the big picture and not on my current situation. Everybody wants to make it, and we all wants to see our dreams come to fruition, but it is critical to remain patient because impetuousness often leads to poor and unethical decisions. For instance, we have had several opportunities to take manufacturing overseas, but we haven't because we don't have enough information about the facilities where our clothing would be manufactured. In addition to being a fraction of the cost, manufacturing overseas would allow Epic Life to push into high production. The only dilemma is that we need to be cautious about the production of our product because it could devastate our integrity. Thus I learned trying to grow too fast may lead to poor and unethical decision making.

Starting a business is a lot of fun but also a lot of hard work. Doing it right and making the right decisions will save a lot of grief and setbacks in the long run. Be sure to be passionate about what you are doing, and give your business 110%.

Chapter Seven

Poll & Flox: Made in the USA

Presented by Félix Poll

Poll & Flox markets innovative clothing

and accessories that the company designs, manufactures, packages, and distributes under its own distinctive brand. This brand is promoted as the symbol of good taste and tuned-in fashion in all current and future products.

I, Félix Poll, created Poll & Flox to combine business with the impulse to design that I've had since I was a child. Born in the mountain town of Utuado, Puerto Rico, I studied aspects of clothing design when and where I could in the United States and Puerto Rico. After brief stints with established designers, I began part-time studies toward a degree in business at the InterAmerican University of Puerto Rico. I had dreamed of creating my own label for a long time, so I used Poll & Flox for a 1997 school project to design and develop a brand name. Before I could design products for manufacture and sale, I needed to position my new brand, and Puerto Rico's small but active fashion industry was a good starting point, at least for the local market. In the long run, my goal was and is to harness Puerto Rico's fashion creativity into a dynamic industry that manufactures locally and exports globally, making Poll & Flox a high-quality international label.

I staged my first fashion show in my hometown in 1998 to benefit a charity, using my contacts in the industry to entice some of the best local professional models (which included my sister) to donate their time and wear my designs. The location of the event was unusual enough to make it noticed and thus started ongoing press coverage. I was able to use the publicity to garner contracts to design gala activities and fashion shows as well as design one-of-a-kind products for major charity events at hotels and museums in San Juan and Ponce, Puerto Rico's two largest cities.

Name recognition grew, and in the fall of 2000, Poll & Flox was asked to help design and develop the concept for Catwalk, an activity promoting up-and-coming fashion designers used to launch Coors Light beer on the island. By the time we set up the second Catwalk in the spring of 2001, the Poll & Flox name was becoming established as a designer brand for the young, upscale population in Puerto Rico. In 2001, I used the Internet to find new technologies to apply to a product. Identifying a "seamless" way of making clothing, where the garment and its elastic are formed from the same material, I made contact with a manufacturer in Italy. They liked the logo and helped me develop the styles for a line of men's underwear, the first Poll & Flox product for the global market. Local manufacturing equipment was outdated, and Italy was too far away, so I returned to the Internet. Once I had identified a manufacturer in the United States, I took my designs and hopped on an airplane to California for a face-to-face meeting. I convinced the manufacturer that the brand and the product had a future, and he agreed to supply samples at cost. I designed packaging and a catalog. Using a top photographer and friend and Puerto Rico's top male model as volunteers (I was the creative director), I was able to combine photography with the logo in eye-catching designs for both packaging and sales materials.

This generated the first sales, and now orders go to California for manufacture. The product ships to Puerto Rico for packaging and then to boutiques in Puerto Rico and New York. Off-island shipping is by container, in which, particularly in outgoing cargo, good pricing can be obtained.

Sales of one-of-a-kind pieces, which I sold to private clients in 2000, grossed approximately $16,000.00. By the end of 2002, I started to work on the seamless program. With the first sales accomplished, I entered the Anheuser-Busch "Lanzate al Futuro" entrepreneurial competition. Poll & Flox won first place for innovation in brand creation, its global business concept, and Poll & Flox Seamless, Puerto Rico's first product with international reach and production capacity from a Puerto Rican designer. This year, Poll & Flox Seamless sales have the potential to reach $1.3 million, based on sales of 96,000 pieces among high-end specialty department stores in the United States alone, and we are already pushing our brand in the international market.

Underwear sales generate close to $4 billion in sales annually. There is very little variety in men's underwear, which accounts for only a fraction of that total amount, making upper-income, fashion conscious males an ideal market for Poll & Flox and a good niche for a newcomer in the fashion world.

The logo is a key element of the brand, and marketing the logo while marketing a product is key to creating an image and setting the stage for future products and growth. The pieces come in a variety of styles and colors, but Poll & Flox logo accents each one. The packaging also highlights the logo and uses brilliant color to catch the eye and a sophisticated "European" look to further distinguish the product for its audience. As a student, I've had to keep costs low (my home computer constitutes my office), but I never rely on anything that affects quality or contradicts the perception of Poll & Flox as a prestigious brand.

I rely on the Internet for sales, research, and communications, and I also use product catalogs, presentations, and shows to sell to buyers. I continue to design one-of-a-kind outfits to keep the Poll & Flox name in the public eye and fashion shows to showcase the image, particularly during Puerto Rico's "fashion week," attended by buyers as well as local and international media. Since many of my individual outfits highlight the Poll & Flox brand name, the print and TV coverage of the ongoing fashion events have been my marketing and publicity tools.

The average cost per clothing item is $5.10. The wholesale prices are between $13 and $15, and retail prices, $25 to $30. This relatively high-priced specialty item -- with both the product and the packaging bearing the Poll & Flox logo -- is ideal for boutique outlets and specialty department stores. Starting as my own salesman, I persuaded as many outlets as possible to try the product, on consignment if necessary. Growing numbers of orders have given me the ammunition to capture the large national retail chains while developing a market that will be ready for future Poll & Flox products. Plans are also in the works to target outlets in Europe and Hong Kong using trade shows such as Intima in New York's Jacob Javits Center. The Internet tells me that more than 2000 buyers, media people, showrooms, and stores from 13 countries attend this event.

As any business owner should, I constantly ponder how much ethics affects my business vision. In my selected industry (fashion), there are several issues that we have to be extremely careful about in order to do what is right. For instance, my biggest challenge was to keep production in the United States instead of moving to China, Mexico, or South America. If we moved production outside the United States, we could get a considerably lower cost and offer a better price to our clients and, consequently, grow faster. However, the financial structure and social conditions of these countries are not healthy. A child in China can work 24 hours and only get 50 cents. In the Dominican Republic, a woman can sew an entire month for $30, and in South America, it can get even worse. I do not want to be successful in the fashion industry exploiting human life. My vision to achieve recognition and have outstanding financial performance is something we want to share with our staff, employees, sponsors, and partners, but our final decision in this ethical issue was to remain as a "Made in the USA" company.

Fashion is somehow an entertainment-related business where you can become famous exploiting your intimate life. This is why I have chosen to keep my life private, yet I still go out of my way to meet people. Because I live in a small quiet town in the middle of the island, distance and language are my first two obstacles. Nobody from a high-end market goes to Utuado for a business meeting, so I used the Internet and conference calls to talk to editors, buyers, and suppliers, and even to send the catalog and other visuals. If I received a request to see a sample, I sent it using Federal Express to get it there in 24 hours.

I speak Spanish, and teaching English is not a priority in my town's schools. This and limited finances made getting training difficult, but I did have the opportunity of training for a year in California, where, with the help of the people I met from around the world, I improved my English enough to make it my "official business language."

After I returned home, I realized that knowing something about business was essential. Focusing on dollars and cents rather than design has been a necessity rather than a pleasure, as has working and studying at the same time. I enrolled at a local university to get a degree in business administration, which I hope to complete in December 2004.

Breaking into the fashion world when you are young and unknown is difficult, and I have spent a great deal of time creating a network of people from Puerto Rico's fashion industry. I worked *pro bono* with other designers and assisted stylists because I believe marketing the Poll & Flox brand is a delicate and ongoing process.

Financing has been an obstacle since nobody trusts an entrepreneur student from a small town with a global business project. The entrepreneurial competitions and recognitions have served to get people interested in Poll & Flox and have brought some money into the project -- not the capital needed, but a few dollars and lots of contacts to keep things moving forward. I am fortunate to be in an industry that appreciates creative concepts and artistic visions. And I can call on the resources available to anyone on the Internet. That is what has enabled me to find the manufacturing facilities in the United States to help me develop a product of unsurpassed quality from the very start to generate the kind of sales and future that I envision for the brand. I see the male seamless line moving out from New York to Europe, Hong Kong, and worldwide, all via customers visiting

www.pollandflox.com. Soon, the company should be marketing a seamless line for women, simultaneously marketing and manufacturing the "Basics" natural fiber underwear. In five years, we will be starting to think about accessories, ready-to-wear, and other related products.

Biographies
of the Entrepreneurs

William
Barrett

Barrett Investment Group

423-791-3843

William Barrett

became an entrepreneur early. In the third grade, he sold cinnamon-oil soaked toothpicks to classmates. Though the enterprise didn't make much money, it was clear that entrepreneurship was in his blood.

As a senior in high school, William noticed a need for specialized cleaning services that catered to sporting events. With his "can do" spirit, he quickly secured cleaning contracts, successfully competing against larger, more established companies. In 2000, William won third place honors regionally in the North American Collegiate Entrepreneur Contest. That same year, he started Waterwood Wonders to diversify. Waterwood Wonders takes worn and weathered tree stumps - driftwood collected from area lakes and converts them into functional works of art for the home. This business won William first place honors regionally in the North American Collegiate Entrepreneur Contest and gave him the opportunity to be a featured writer in the first edition of Student Entrepreneurs.

William continued to think big, and in 2001 he started BIG, the Barrett Investment Group. BIG is a real-estate investment company specializing in residential development. A 2004 college graduate, William is now focused more than ever on his businesses.

Brian Bushell

Memory Foam Factory

Brian@memoryfoamfactory.com

Memory Foam Factory
61 Kuller Rd.
Clifton, NJ 07015

(877) MEM-FOAM (Phone)
(877) 636-3626

Brian Bushell

grew up in Hillsdale, New Jersey, a small town outside Manhattan. Brian was never interested in school for conventional reasons. He was all about learning the ropes in hopes that one day he would be in charge of the ropes. Somewhere along the way, Brian decided it would be more effective to apply his intelligence and creativity to something constructive, and entrepreneurship was a perfect fit.

Brian grew up in a family with three passions: food, business, and golf. He believes the long hours he spent on the golf course as a young man have been extremely influential in his early success with his first venture, the Memory Foam Factory. Golf requires an unusual combination of patience, concentration, resolve, and humility. Brian was lucky enough to grow up playing the game with many of New Jersey's most successful businessmen, doctors, lawyers, and bankers.

Brian started the Memory Foam Factory in the summer between his junior and senior years at Syracuse University. After trying out a few prototypes for himself and performing some very cursory and informal market research on the Syracuse campus, Brian knew he had a valuable product and could generate a profit from its efficient distribution. After building an e-commerce website, and learning through trial and error the most effective ways to market his products, the Memory Foam Factory has grown at a rate that would make any Fortune 500 CEO proud.

Ahmad Fouda

Rook's Events

www.wildcats.com.au

jerricho73@hotmail.com

(61) 0439972724 (phone)

Ahmad Fouda

was born in Bankstown, Sydney, Australia, the oldest of four children. From early childhood he had a great passion for both the sport of basketball and anything related to aviation. The family moved to Perth in the early 90s, and Ahmad began pursuing his goal of becoming a pilot while his passion for basketball grew stronger.

In 2000, Ahmad was accepted to study Aviation at Edith Cowan University. His idea for Rook's 3on3 Basketball came during the middle of spring 2002 when he witnessed the decline of the amateur basketball games he so enjoyed. Rook's is centered on promoting and running amateur basketball competitions with the goal of branching out to set up a franchise operation and have a league of its own.

Ahmad also runs seminars that encourage young people to start their own business or social enterprise. The goals of these seminars are to build the confidence and capacity of young people to help themselves and their community. In its first two years, the basketball competition grew to include a large number of youth from differing communities and sent a message of hope and help to the youngsters of Australia.

Even though big competitors have again flooded the market with amateur basketball contests, the future for Rook's looks bright with outstanding networking opportunities. Ahmad is proud to have raised the profile of a struggling sport in Australia.

Social Impact Winner

Narcedalia Lozano
Garza

La Paz Comienza
con los Niños

www.lapaz.org.mx

info@lapaz.org.mx

Narcedalia Lozano Garza

was born in Monterrey, Mexico, on July 21, 1979. Her family is mother Narcedalia de Lozano, father Gilberto Lozano, brothers Gilberto, Carlos, and Javier, and her husband Juan Moisés Perales. Narcedalia attended high school at the Preparatoria Eugenio Garza Sada. In addition to being president of the alumni society, she graduated with honors in 1997. In 1995, she represented Mexico in the World Leadership Congress in Boston, Massachusetts, and went to the Odyssey of the Mind World Finals 1996 in Des Moines, Iowa. She studied English at Saint Mary's University of Minnesota in 1997 and went on to study economics and major in International Relations at Monterrey Tech (ITESM), graduating with honors in June 2003.

During her studies, she was a member of the TEC Chamber Orchestra playing the flute. She went to Stanford University and represented Mexico in the International Symposium for Mediation and Conflict Resolution in Belgium and the Netherlands in 1999. In 2000 she founded a non-profit organization called La Paz Comienza con los Niños, running music workshops for the children of Casa Paterna La Gran Familia. In 2001, she legally established the foundation and it began to expand both in numbers of volunteers and participating children. She received the 2002 National Prize for Community Social Service from the Secretary of Social Development (SEDESOL), the 2003 Global Student Entrepreneur Award for Social Impact from Saint Louis University, and was named 2003 Student of the Year by EXP and the Coca-Cola Company. In 2004, she began an enterprise in the educational field that will contribute to the growth of La Paz Comienza con los Niños.

Matthew
Hinson

Wake Works Staffing

www.wakeworks.com

mhinson@wakeworks.com

Matthew Hinson

is a serial entrepreneur. After numerous childhood business endeavors, he produced his first sustainable company in 1998 at the age of 16. Cyberian Solutions provided consulting on emerging technologies to businesses across the Washington D.C. area. The company was essentially "unfinished business" as Matt left the D.C. area to attend Wake Forest University. Matt was attracted to Wake Forest's interest in promoting entrepreneurial activities and its emphasis on innovation.

Matt was struck with the inspiration for Wake Works during the end of his freshman year. He was working as a waiter at a local hotel and was appalled by the quality of the temporary labor. After researching the market, Matt approached the hotel's general manager with the Wake Works concept: a company able to provide highly trained employees on relatively short notice. The manager hesitantly agreed to give the concept a trial run, and Wake Works Staffing, Inc. was born.

Since its inception Wake Works Staffing, Inc. has grown exponentially, and is currently the premier staffing agency in western North Carolina. The corporation engages approximately 160 Wake Workers to serve as temporary servers, bartenders, and valet parkers for the area's most discerning clientele. Matt recently launched a licensing initiative with entrepreneurs at Princeton and Vanderbilt and hopes to expand the Wake Works concept to additional campuses within the next year.

2003 Global Collegiate Entrepreneur

Joseph
Keeley

College Nannies & Tutors, Inc.

www.collegenannies.com

joe@collegenannies.com

PO Box 213
Wayzata, MN 55391

952-476-0613 (phone)

Joseph Keeley

founded College Nannies & Tutors (originally known as College Summer Nannies) during his sophomore year at the University of St. Thomas in St. Paul, Minnesota, after a rewarding summer as a nanny for a family in the Twin Cities. Joseph spent his summer as a "big brother" of sorts to two boys and a little girl, providing a helping hand with their activities, and yes, even serving as an occasional swimming buddy at the pool! He saw the business potential of connecting working parents interested in a "different type of childcare" with his peers at the university who he thought would make excellent "Active Role Models℠" for children after school and during the summer months. College Nannies & Tutors began connecting busy families with college students as nannies in February 2001 in the Minneapolis-St. Paul area. The company has since expanded its services, developed its business infrastructure, and recently began efforts to franchise the concept in order to make a positive difference in the lives of children, parents, and nannies across the United States.

Joseph graduated magna cum laude from the College of Business at the University of St. Thomas in St. Paul with a degree in Entrepreneurship in 2003. In addition to his full time commitment of growing College Nannies & Tutors, Joseph is dedicated to helping foster entrepreneurship in young people. He plans to share his valuable experiences as a student entrepreneur with others through mentoring, speaking, and eventually teaching.

Eric
Knopf

Epic Life, LLC

www.epic-life.com

5291 Dixon Ave. W.
Dixon, CA 95620

877-528-6248 (phone)

Eric Knopf

grew up in Troutdale, Oregon, and has always participated in extreme sports. His parents weren't as enthusiastic, but supported him in everything he did including drawing, computer graphics, guitar, piano, and singing.

While pursuing a motocross-racing career, he took a substantial position as a marketing director for a local motocross company. In addition to marketing, extreme sports, and other activities he was involved in, Eric had a passion for his Christian faith but never thought that he could meld the two interests. It took a devastating motocross racing accident in which a close friend was paralyzed to ignite Eric's determination to create a way to infiltrate pop-culture with a message of faith.

It all started soon after he enrolled at Westmont College in Santa Barbara, California. His entrepreneurial drive first manifested itself in a small organization called The Flood. This non-profit organization put on an evangelistic event targeting today's pop culture with the message of the Gospel. Hundreds of people attended the event, solidifying Eric's ambitions to continue his mission. Two months later in January 2002, Eric created Epic Life, an evangelistic "company" in the form of a clothing manufacturer that sponsors extreme sports, athletes, bands, concerts, and events, and creates media to influence pop-culture for Christ. Using Eric's marketing background, this unique "stealth evangelism" progressed throughout California, developing several partnerships to reach modern culture. Today Eric and Epic Life are still impacting the lives of today's youth in ways never done before.

Adam
Makos

Ghost Wings Magazine

www.Ghostwings.com

staff@ghostwings.com

1004 Yeagle Road
Montoursville, PA 17754

Adam Makos

was motivated by his grandfathers' stories of WWII service.
At an early age, Adam decided to serve American veterans
by preserving their history. While in the 8th grade, long before
anyone was taking much notice of the "Greatest Generation",
Adam created the *Ghost Wings Newsletter*. The circular was
named after a WWII bomber that vanished while in flight,
like a ghost. In just five years, the newsletter evolved into an
internationally circulated quarterly magazine called *Ghost Wings*.

The magazine's mission has remained constant. *Ghost Wings*
preserves and presents the accounts of veterans who have served in
peacetime and in war, from WWII to the present. Adam, an Eagle
Scout, hopes that Americans of all ages will learn from these stories
that our freedoms were forged through great sacrifice.

A recent college graduate with marketing and communication
degrees, Adam pursues his business full-time. His career
accomplishments are varied. He shot film used on the
NBC Nightly News, piloted a WWII bomber, gave testimony in
Washington on behalf of the WWII Memorial, and served as
vice-president of media relations for famed pilot General
Chuck Yeager. Adam's work was recently published in the
Royal Aeronautical Society Journal alongside authors such as
Joint Chiefs Chairman Richard Meyers.

Encouraged to pursue a writing career by the late renowned
historian Steven Ambrose, Adam has started his first book
and intends to preserve a part of American history that will
make his grandfathers proud.

Miles
Mays

Flying M Livestock, LLC

5323 Wilson Creek Road
Ellensburg, WA 98926

Miles Mays

was born and raised in Ellensburg, Washington, on a cattle ranch. Ranch life instilled Miles with a "do-it-yourself" attitude, and also taught him the importance and value of hard work.

In 1994, Miles' father seized an opportunity to expand the family business by taking in yearling cattle from Hawaii. Hawaii has no commercial feedlots or slaughterhouses, so cattle are shipped to the mainland to be grass-fed. Before long, containers full of cattle were arriving by the truckload to graze the pastures of the Crooked Arrow Ranch. After unloading, the empty truck containers needed to be washed.

Miles and his brothers were challenged to design a truck washout system that was both efficient and profitable, and they were rewarded with a new business: Flying M Washout. In its initial year, the washout machine used one pump to clean 54 containers. By 1999 the number of containers increased to more than 100, and the washout was completely overhauled. The new washout uses a more complex wastewater drainage system and a top-of-the-line pumping scheme. Miles' continuing education in dynamic fluid mechanics and water resource management has been critical to the success of the washout system.

Profits from Flying M Washout allowed Miles and his brothers to expand into the livestock sector in 2001, creating Flying M Livestock, LLC. They purchased 88 purebred cows to pasture on their family's ranch and now own 120 head of beef cattle.

Chiquita
Miller-Nolan

Royal Touch Salon Plus

chiquita_nolan@yahoo.com

20003 Timber Forest Drive
Humble, TX 77346

281-852-3755 (phone)

Chiquita Miller~Nolan

is the wife of Pastor Ronald W. Nolan and proud mother of daughters, Quiese, Quiedra, and son, Isaac. Chiquita has the responsibility of balancing her family, business, ministry, and school all at the same time.

Entrepreneurship is not new to Chiquita. She comes from a family with a strong entrepreneurial background. Working for her mother, Minnie Miller, a veteran at starting, building, and maintaining successful businesses, Chiquita developed her own "business sense".

She began Royal Touch Salon Plus in 1997 as a Christian owned and operated business. It is unique in that it maintains a family atmosphere. RTSP was the first of its kind in the Atascocita area of Humble, Texas. There were other salons but none with a vision like this one. This salon was designed from the outset to serve men, women, and children of all races in one location.

Chiquita returned to school in 2002 to major in Business Management. She graduated in 2004 from Kingwood College in Kingwood, Texas, and is now a licensed cosmetologist, certified master stylist, and a chemical and weave specialist. She is also an ordained minister and licensed evangelist. She won first place in the Arklatex Region (Arkansas, Louisiana, & Texas) of the Global Student Entrepreneur Awards. Chiquita has been able to combine ministry and work by not only fixing hair, but also fixing lives.

James
Nicholas

JE 2000, LLC

www.je2000.com

jnicholas@je2000.com

James Nicholas

has always had an entrepreneurial drive. From the age of nine, James had businesses ranging from selling baseball cards to cutting lawns to shoveling snow. As a sophomore in high school, he started a small web development business, JE2000, LLC. Just a few years later, it was a global web hosting company with over 235 customers in more than ten countries. James propelled the company to double its revenue in each of the first five years. He grew the company by providing superior and personal customer service. Moreover, James listened to his customers to understand their needs exactly, and then he provided a service to fulfill those needs.

James graduated magna cum laude from Bryant College in Smithfield, Rhode Island, with a Bachelor's of Business Administration with dual concentrations in computer information systems and communications. He earned the Bryant College Student Entrepreneur of the Year Award and first place in the business plan competition. He developed many valuable relationships through the program and learned about philanthropy as a major part of any successful business.

During the summer, James enjoys playing as much golf as possible. He also loves to read myriad books focusing on business and personal growth.

Innovation Award Winner

Felix
Poll

Poll & Fox

www.pollandflox.com

felix@pollandflox.com

P.O. Box 892
Utuado, Puerto Rico 00641-0892

787-627-8780 (Puerto Rico phone)
212-244-2377 (New York phone)

Felix Poll

grew up in Utuado, Puerto Rico. After high school, he moved to
Los Angeles, where he enrolled in an intense fashion program. He
combined fashion with fine arts and completed his studies at
The Pontified Catholic University of Puerto Rico. He later
moved to New York to study marketing and publicity.

Long before completing his studies, Felix began working in
Puerto Rico in the creative departments of high fashion designers.
He was also teaching part-time at the Instituto de Diseño y Moda de
Carlota Alfaro, the most prestigious fashion design institute in
Puerto Rico. He developed amazing pattern making techniques
and advanced clothing engineering skills.

In 1998, Felix made a major career move when he decided to start
working on his own label. He turned a clever mix of his last name
and a family nickname into one of the hottest new labels on the
island: Poll & Flox. To complete his label concept, Felix designed
a unique logo that is the focal point and accent of his
clothing and accessory creations.

The combination of technology, sophisticated yarns, great cuts,
sexy silhouettes, colors, the logo accents, and handcrafted
techniques became the distinctive look of Poll & Flox pieces.
Within a few short years the label began to achieve recognition in
fashion industry magazines, newspapers, and even television reviews.

With Poll & Flox, Felix has won several entrepreneur
competitions and achieved recognition in Puerto Rico, the U.S., and
around the world including "Exito Empresarial Universitario"
awarded by the International Entrepreneur Institute of Puerto Rico
and *El Nuevo Dia* Newspaper; Anheuser-Busch & Budweiser
Entrepreneur Competition for $10,000.00; and the
Global Student Entrepreneur[SM] Award for Innovation,
awarded by Saint Louis University.

Matt
Staver

Matthew Staver Photography

www.mattstaver.com

Matt Staver

got his professional career got off to an early start. By the beginning of his sophomore year at Colorado State University, Matt had a news photograph splashed on the front page of the *Denver Post*, one of the 10 largest newspapers in the country.

Since then he has been published in the *Wall Street Journal*, the *New York Times*, the *Washington Post* and the *Philadelphia Inquirer*. He has photographed women hunters for a spread in *Jane Magazine*, taken pictures for *Time Magazine,* and had a photograph spanning two pages in *Sports Illustrated on Campus*. Regular photography gigs include chasing wildfires for the *Denver Post* and photographing sports for the United States Air Force Academy. He's even had his photos made into a calendar.

Staver graduated cum laude from CSU in 2001 with a Bachelor's in Business Administration, and immediately moved to Denver to continue developing Matthew Staver Photography. When not on assignment in Colorado he takes every opportunity to see the world. He has sent himself on assignment to shoot volcanoes in Ecuador, monks in Thailand, and boxers in Cuba. When not behind the lens, Matt enjoys rock climbing, running, and seeing just how many hours he can go without sleep.

Andrew
Szatko

Grassroots Landscaping, INC

www.gralandscaping.net

4729 S. 81st St
Omaha, NE 68127

402-306-5704 (phone)

Andrew Szatko

was born in 1980 in Omaha, Nebraska. At the age of seven,
he was in a severe thunderstorm, and announced he wanted to
become a meteorologist/storm chaser. But in 1997, he took a job at
a landscape and nursery company where he found a new passion.

Andy began his freshman year studying meteorology but quickly
switched to horticulture and landscape design because of his love of
working in the outdoors. The summer after his freshman year,
Andy created Grassroots Landscaping, Inc. Andy saw that he could
provide a service to his clients that would stand out among the many
other landscaping companies. As Grassroots Landscaping grew, he
had to manage both the company and his college classes. His studies
paid off when, in the spring of 2003, he won first place regionally in
the Global Student Entrepreneurship Awards. That same year he
graduated with his degree in Horticulture
and married his wife, Melissa.

Andy continues to grow his business with lawn care, landscape
design and construction as the company's main services. The business
became a family affair in 2003 when Andy's father joined it to offer
custom carpentry of arbors, bridges, chairs, and other
hardscape elements to their clients.

Regional Partners

The Entrepreneurship Center
Seattle University
Harriet Stephenson
Albers School of Business & Economics
900 Broadway
Seattle, Washington 98122-4340
206/296-5730
ec@seattleu.edu

Loyola Marymount University
Fred Kiesner
1112 Snowbird Drive
Frazier Park, California 93225
310/338-4569
fkiesner@lmu.edu or himself@frazmtn.com

Nebraska Center for Entrepreneurship
University of Nebraska--Lincoln
Elaine Warren
CBA 209
Lincoln, Nebraska 68588-0487
402/472-3353
ewarren2@unl.edu

Rothman Institute of Entrepreneurial Studies
Fairleigh Dickinson University
James Barrood
285 Madison Ave.
Madison, New Jersey 07940
973/443-8887
Barrood@fdu.edu

Harold E. Anderson Entrepreneurial Center
St. Cloud State University
Ken Maddux
616 Roosevelt Rd., Suite 100
St. Cloud, Minnesota 56301
320/654-5420
kmaddux@stcloudstate.edu

Jefferson Smurfit Center for Entrepreneurial Studies
Saint Louis University
Sharon Bower
Cook School of Business 3674 Lindell Ave.
St. Louis, Missouri 63108
314/977-3896
bowersk@slu.edu

College of Business Administration
University of Texas / El Paso
Frank Hoy
El Paso, Texas 79968-0545
915/747-7727
fhoy@utep.edu

Muldoon Center for Entrepreneurship
John Carroll University
Dianne Welsh
Boler School of Business 20700 N Park Blvd.
University Heights, Ohio 44118-4581
216/397-4970
dwelsh@jcu.edu

International Entrepreneurship Institute
Guarionex #12 Ponce de Leon
José Romaguera
Mayaguez, Puerto Rico 00680 USA
787/833-7254
emprende@coqui.net

St. FX Enterprise Development Centre
Tiiu Poder
PO Box 5000
Antigonish, NS B2G 2W5 CANADA
902/867-2211
tpoder@stfx.ca

RMIT School of Management
RMIT University
Kathy Griffiths
16/239 Bourke St.
Melbourne, Victoria 3000 AUSTRALIA
61-3-9925-5940
kathryn.griffiths@rmit.edu.au

Swedish Foundation for Small Business Research
Fakultetsgatan 1
Britt-Marie Nordström
Örebro, 701 82 SWEDEN
46-705-629-633
britt-marie.nordstrom@esi.oru.se

Chapter 8

Beyond the Bottom Line

Presented by Matt Hinson

I am a habitual entrepreneur. Although I have

formed three successful ventures over the past eight years, I never sit down and plan to start a company. All three of my companies have evolved from confronting a simple problem or problems and searching for a basic solution. In the past eight years, I have encountered successes and failures, awards, audits, and lawsuits. Through it all, I have determined one simple fact: at the end of the day, a person's honor is his or her most valuable asset.

In the Beginning…

From a young age, I have encountered companies that did not respect their employees and belittled individuals based solely on their age or appearance. At the age of 16, I started a computer consulting company, Cyberian Solutions, which provided emerging technology consulting to organizations in the Washington D.C. area. Throughout my tenure with Cyberian Solutions, I was struck by the frequent "prejudgments" made based solely upon my age. One instance that was particularly striking involved an initial bid meeting with a perspective client. The meeting was arranged based on a referral from a current client who touted our innovation and efficiency. When I arrived for the meeting, I was introduced to the company's president, who promptly inquired, "When is your boss showing up?" I quickly informed him that I was the company representative and would gladly assist him to the best of my ability. The president promptly declined our services, claiming that he feared our "youthful" exterior. However talented and full of potential a company is, today's business world equates age with ability, and this is the stereotype young entrepreneurs will always fight.

Still, through my many successes, I have learned that while youth is frequently equated with irresponsibility and immaturity, it should never serve as a deterrent to entering the business world. Entering the marketplace as a young individual brings with it certain responsibilities. Young entrepreneurs wage daily battles against ingrained stereotypes that call not only our proficiency but also our integrity into question. The prevalence of these stereotypes demands that we hold ourselves to a higher moral standard. We must conduct our business as though we are under a microscope. This constant scrutiny is eventually advantageous as it frequently sparks an outpouring of support from the business community once a young entrepreneur's moral caliber and work ethic become established. In our case, when Wake Works landed its first major account and began producing significant revenue, we piqued the interest of investors and the media. To our surprise, their interest was not in our business model or level of services but rather in the fact that we operated our organization with integrity at the forefront, and that we consistently delivered on our promises.

Peas and Carrots

When I conceived of Wake Works, I recruited a business partner, David Willhoit, who served as my support and advocate during the trying times of the corporation's first 18 months of operation. David managed the company's employee relations and event fulfillment, while I oversaw day-to-day administration: AP/AR (Accounts Purchasing/ Accounts Receivables) client relations, and business development. I specifically recruited David because of his magnetic personality and social nature. David was able to maintain relationships with our then 80 employees and knew each by name. David excelled where I was weaker, possessing the interpersonal skills needed to effectively manage our "human capital," while I refined the organization's focus and concentrated on business development.

Socrates once said that "a wise man knows what he does not know." I have been continually taught that lesson over that past few years. While David and I were polar opposites in most respects, our divergent personalities created a symbiotic relationship that bred success. Our complimentary personalities allowed "two guys and a dorm room" to manage an employee pool of 100 individuals and a client list that included the area's largest establishments. My interactions with David taught me that to achieve success you need to surround yourself with individuals who excel where you often fail. After several months, the volume of our business necessitated additional staffers to assist David and me in the company's day-to-day activities. I did not simply hire "assistants" but rather analyzed our current skill set and determined several operational holes within the company. Once these holes were discovered, I was able to approach MBA students from the Wake Forest's Babcock School of Management about openings within the company. This method of staff assembly lends itself to true team-building. Each individual works to the best of his or her ability for good of the whole company, and everyone benefits.

Hiring and Firing...The World of Pink Slips

The methodology behind Wake Works' employee hiring process was similar to our efforts at building an executive team. When hiring employees, we adopted a holistic approach, evaluating each applicant as an individual rather than as a revenue stream or a labor unit. Most temporary agencies assess applicants based on their skill set and experience in the industry of application. Wake Works abandoned traditional assessment tools. Instead, we chose to evaluate employees based on their past pursuits because looking at their interests exhibited their passions and leadership abilities. In the end, skill sets are learned, but passion and drive are innate character traits that can change the face of your staff. Because we commonly hired individuals with little industry experience, training became a central focus. Wake Works has developed a server-training program, which holds a "baptism by fire" mentality. New employees attend an initial classroom session where they receive instruction in serving skills and basic etiquette. Trainees are then placed with a mentor for hands-on training. While hiring employees with little experience increased workforce acquisition costs, the level of overall competency and trust associated with employing persons of character was invaluable.

As I mentioned earlier, young entrepreneurs are evaluated stringently by the business community at large. As a result, each action, client engagement, and strategic move must be conducted with the utmost attention to detail and integrity of action. Because the nature of our business requires that we maintain a significant labor pool, strict quality controls are implemented to ensure adherence to company standards.

To assist in our quality control endeavors, I adopted the philosophy of 10%, which was first introduced by General Electric in the 1980s. At the end of each semester, the entire staffing pool undergoes an impartial evaluation in which the bottom 10% of the pool is either removed from payroll or required to attend additional training. To remain impartial in this evaluation, I commissioned a piece of statistical analysis software that allowed event managers to log in and evaluate each employee after an event. At the end of each semester, the application produces a list of the lowest performing employees who are then either re-admitted to our training program or released from service. By consciously managing the quality of an organization's output, it is possible for past results to be indicative of future performance. Due to our consistent quality standards, clients had an assurance that every labor order would be filled by competent, professional staffers.

One of the most difficult tasks for student entrepreneurs can be learning how to effectively terminate employees. This task proved especially daunting as many of my employees were peers. While the use of employee evaluation software added an element of impartiality to our employee review/termination process, the task is never an easy one. After several difficult termination meetings, I decided that firm company guidelines and full disclosure from the initial hiring would ensure the most painless termination process. From the moment employees join Wake Works, every interaction they have with the company is documented in writing, and when individuals are flagged as a bottom 10% performer, they enter a standardized employee evaluation process. Each "at risk" employee attends a counseling session with a company manager where they are allowed to view their performance reports, ask questions, and have their options presented to them in a non-confrontational manner. At-risk employees can either opt to be dropped from the corporate labor pool or attend an additional training session in an attempt to improve their serving skills. The standardization of disciplinary procedures allows administrators to feel that they are serving the best interests of both the organization and the individual employee.

Don't Reinvent the Wheel

Young entrepreneurs frequently enter markets with a certain naiveté concerning the basic operating principles of the business world. The youthful inexperience that breeds this naiveté can be a valuable driving force behind much of the zeal young entrepreneurs exude. The young entrepreneur's ability to see through roadblocks, often operating ventures with disregard for traditional safety nets, allows for both high rates of success and failure. Young entrepreneurs must identify their competitive advantage early on and make that single issue their primary focus in order to overcome the significant pressures -- financial and otherwise -- that accompany any business venture. For example, soon after Wake Works was conceived, we received inquires from several local businesses seeking to form joint ventures using our labor pool. These suggestions varied from nanny and tutoring services to landscaping teams. While several of the companies offered to invest the capital needed for the ventures, we refused the alliances, fearing that they would dilute our competitive advantage in the marketplace. Allowing an immature venture to grow in varied paths without experience and significant capital resources can impair the company's scalability in the long term. Concentrating effort on a singular goal increases a business concept's chances of survival by limiting the number of issues vying for the entrepreneur's attention.

College campuses are unique environments in which some of the most talented young minds in the country are centrally concentrated and seeking a chance to prove their skills. Soon after the company's formation, I faced the daunting task of creating a corporate infrastructure that was both functional and simple; to achieve this task, I delegated as much work as possible. For example, an art major created the company's logo, a local MBA candidate created our initial marketing plan, and computer science majors developed several custom software applications. All of these tasks were completed with professional quality at a very low cost. College campuses are brimming with such untapped potential, so if you need help, ask.

Soon after starting Wake Works, I realized that to operate a business on a large scale, we would need the services of both accountants and lawyers to ensure that we remained compliant with the myriad of state and federal regulations. With little capital available, I approached several local law and accounting firms and explained our startup's limited resources. I was amazed that many of these firms were willing to provide services pro bono due to their respect for our venture. The fact that collegiate entrepreneurs are so intrinsically different from the stereotypical student actually works in our favor and frequently translates directly into free or reduced cost professional services. Currently, all of our legal and accounting services are provided at or below cost, providing the corporation with a professional safety net in times of trouble. When starting a business, consistently ask for help until you find someone willing to provide it.

Between a Rock and a Hard Place

In its first two and a half years of operation, Wake Works faced significant roadblocks. We experienced threats from competitors, financial hardships, inquiries by the IRS, and stiff competition from national staffing agencies in the area. Through all of these confrontations, the one aspect of the corporation which was not challenged was our integrity. If you conduct your business dealings with a long-term goal at the forefront, the risk of personal loss is exponentially decreased.

Money is always a sensitive subject among entrepreneurs; it is frequently in short supply and rarely in excess. When designing Wake Works, I took a rather nontraditional stance in composing the revenue model. Instead of attempting to maximize profit, our goal became to maximize experience. Wake Works is designed both as a fully functioning corporation and as a training ground for young entrepreneurs. The fact that Wake Works allows college students to gain real-world management and administrative experience while still in college attracts some of the brightest collegiate minds in the area to its executive team. Because the majority of our employees are students, we actively attempt to minimize the revenue percentage taken from employees, thus placing a cap on possible profits. While this theory goes against fundamental tenants of capitalism, it speaks to a larger issue. Wake Works is intended to be an educational experience providing flexible employment, high wages, and management experience to college-age individuals. While the corporation certainly produces a profit for its shareholders, we strive to place the experience ahead of the bottom line.

This mentality is also reflected in our corporate culture. Wake Works makes every effort not only to provide a fair working wage but also to give back to our workers and the community at large. In August of 2002, we created a Wake Works Employee Scholarship that is issued twice a year and covers the cost of both books and school supplies for a deserving employee. Additionally, we sponsor a community service event once a semester, which is open to all employees. These events typically involve service at a local soup kitchen or a program for underprivileged children. By supporting our employees in their academic endeavors and encouraging our staff to remain active in the community, we attempt to create a culture that rewards performance, values passion, and encourages integrity.

The Future

Wake Works began a franchising initiative in August of 2003 after receiving significant interest from entrepreneurs at Vanderbilt and Princeton. I decided to license the business model to like-minded college students across the country in an attempt to propagate the values and ideals that allow the corporation to function so smoothly. When I was a child, my father would frequently read me poetry by Rudyard Kipling. Kipling's poem "If" has served as an inspiration to me throughout my entrepreneurial career and continues to embody my interpretation of honor. The poem is a father's definition of integrity to his son and states that a true man is the embodiment of honor and passion:

> If you can fill the unforgiving minute
> With sixty seconds' worth of distance run,
> Yours is the Earth and everything that's in it,
> And-which is more-you'll be a Man, my son!

Chapter Nine

The FEATS of Success

Presented by James Nicholas

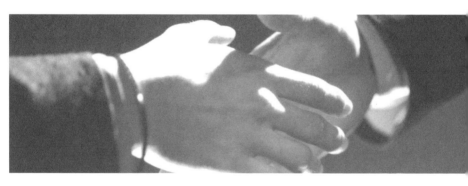

For me, becoming an entrepreneur started at
a very young age. While in elementary school, during the winter
months, I would wax my snow shovel before an expected storm. If
school was cancelled, or it was a weekend and a storm came, I would
go door to door in my neighborhood and shovel snow. I also learned
at a very early age how to negotiate. During the summers, I would
walk my lawn mower up to a half mile away from my home to cut
lawns. While cutting lawns, I learned about customer service. Not
only did I cut the lawn, but I weed-whacked and removed any grass
clippings from the driveway and sidewalk. The little extra time it
took to provide a better service paid off. I received more word-of-
mouth referrals, and my customer retention rate was a perfect 100%.
I realized that these businesses were seasonal, so I attempted to sell
baseball cards at shows during my "off season." This was not very
profitable and was failure number one. However, I learned how to
deal with people. Next, I tried to sell how-to manuals through classi-
fied advertising, which proved to be failure number two. From this
venture, I learned that making money is not easy. Subsequently, I
began selling air purifiers. Again, I failed. However, I did learn how
important it is to research the product, marketplace, competition,
and price before investing a lot of money into a product. In short, I
failed numerous times, but I learned from every one of my failures.
Therefore, none of these experiences were really failures because I
learned from my mistakes.

As a sophomore in high school, I decided to develop websites. During
Christmas vacation, I picked up the local yellow pages and called
businesses to find out if they were interested in a website. After
about a 250 calls, I found a potential customer that wanted me to

come into his jewelry store to discuss a possible website. Since I was only 15 years old, my mother had to drive me to the jewelry store. She waited over two hours in the car. Her wait was well worth it, as I walked out of the store with a check. I had my first client at the age of 15.

As I developed the jewelry store's website, I realized I would need to purchase Web hosting, which is space on the Internet, so people could view his site. I figured I should become a vendor of hosting so that I could earn recurring income. Therefore, I also sold my customer Web hosting.

In running my business for over six years, I have discovered that a successful entrepreneur possesses magnificent qualities. I describe some of the characteristics of flourishing entrepreneurs with the word FEATS, which means achievements:

F - Friendly

An entrepreneur must be friendly to everyone. If someone is not a customer, a smart entrepreneur will still be friendly because that person may know a potential customer. One key to being an entrepreneur is building relationships. The easiest way to build relationships is to be friendly to people. If people like you, they will want to give your company business.

Additionally, providing friendly proactive customer service is vital to having a thriving company. Even if your company sells a product, superior customer service will set you apart from the competition. If you can be proactive with customer support, people will be more pleased with your service. As a result, they will refer more people to your business.

In the hosting business, I am as proactive and friendly as possible. If I know of scheduled maintenance, I will notify my customers well in advance of the expected downtime. Then, customers can prepare for the downtime and know that the downtime is only for a short period, which will make their hosting service better. You may even get increased sales when you notify customers because it will put your company name in front of them. They will know that you are still out there. By being friendly, your customer retention rate, repeat business, and referrals will be much higher.

E - Ethical

Entrepreneurs who are honest, ethical, and sincere to their customers will get more business. Being ethical is part of being friendly. Entrepreneurs must always look for the best interest of the customer. If your company offers multiple versions of the same product or service, you should always try to sell the right service or product that fits the customer's needs. If you recommend a lower priced item that suits their needs, customers will respect and trust you. They will feel comfortable in doing business with you and will refer more customers to you.

The Web hosting business is very competitive. At the time of this publication, there are over 200 million Web hosts throughout the world. Price is a major factor in retaining business and getting new customers. In 2003, my business leveled off, and I was not growing at 100% like I was in previous years. I did my competitive analysis and found that my prices were a little higher than most. I decided I had to lower my prices to remain in business.

However, the next decision was whether I should notify my customers of the lower rates or have them find out on their own. The decision was easy. If I were a customer of my company, I would want the lower rate. Furthermore, I would be very appreciative if the owner of the company notified me of the lower rate. In fact, I would be more likely to talk highly of the company and give more referrals. For some, this decision would be difficult because I projected to lose around $10,000 in revenue due to the lower prices. Conversely, I had faith in my hosting service that my company would make up the $10,000 and more with lower prices by attracting new customers and retaining old ones. I had to make an ethical decision in being proactive to my customers and notifying them of the price decrease. I found that if you are ethical, not only will you be more confident in your company, but your customers will trust you and refer more clients to your business.

A - Ambitious

A terrific entrepreneur has to be ambitious. An entrepreneur must be proactive and be willing to do the little extras that will make customers happy. For instance, follow-up phone calls truly impress people and take just minutes to do. Plus, follow-up phone calls are free marketing to your customers. Your customers will feel content that they purchased from your company and not XYZ Company, where they are just a number to the bottom line.

Another example of being ambitious is taking the extra effort to make your storefront, office, or online website look aesthetically pleasing. If you have a storefront or have an office, you should make it look clean, neat, and organized. Having a tidy locale is a good impression to your clients.

If you have a website, you should make sure you choose colors that make the text easy to read. Almost 40% of men are color blind. You should make sure your site has colors on it that are easy to read because if you don't, you could be losing 40% of the male market. Furthermore, your site should be well planned and easy to navigate.

If you sell a service or product on your website, you should conduct a usability test to improve the site's ease of use for the end customer. Usability tests can cost thousands of dollars. However, you do not have to pay this much money to see the major flaws in your site's design. If you sit with five different people and have them place an order on your site, or at least try to, you will see if they complete the process correctly and without difficulty. If you find people are clicking the wrong button or not correctly placing their order, you know that you should move the button to a more obvious location so that the customer can easily place orders on your website. Running an informal usability test is an example of doing the little extras that will allow more customers to order on your website without problems. Another little extra that is important to a lucrative company is to send thank you notes. Sending thank you notes is an affordable way to show your customers that you truly appreciate their business. Also, it gives your business more advertising to the customer. The customer will be more secure with doing business with your company. In short, by being ambitious and doing the little extras, your customers will be happier, which will lead to higher revenues for your company. In short, an ambitious entrepreneur will do the little things to make their customers happy.

T - Task Orientated (Time Management)

Lucrative entrepreneurs must manage their time well. Efficient entrepreneurs will have a task list. Effective entrepreneurs will break up their tasks into categories and prioritize tasks within each category. There are many different time management methods out there. You will have to experiment with different methods and create a system that fits your mindset and needs the best.

Personally, I break up my tasks in daily, weekly, monthly, and long-term categories. I even write down tasks I have completed so I can cross them out and gain a sense of accomplishment. At the beginning of each day, I conquer the most important daily tasks first. Once I have completed my daily tasks, I will move on to the weekly tasks and so on.

Furthermore, if you have one big task that may take a long time, you should break up those big tasks into smaller manageable chunks. Then, break up those small chunks into even smaller tasks. You will be able to manage the overall project easier and be less overwhelmed. If you have numerous jobs to do, when you write them down, they do not look half as bad to tackle. You will find that you get more done in less amount of time with a task list.

S - Savvy

Entrepreneurs must be savvy about everything including their company, product/service, customers, competition, and the overall market. Entrepreneurs must know about their companies' important financials at all times. For example, knowing your company's cash flow is crucial to running a successful business, especially in its early stages. Additionally, the entrepreneur must know about other financial statements, such as the balance sheet and income statement. If you use an accounting program such as QuickBooks or Peachtree, the software will generate these reports with a click of a button. The more you know about the company, the easier it will be to strategize for future growth.

Furthermore, entrepreneurs must be savvy about their own products and services. The more knowledgeable entrepreneurs are about their products and services, the easier these are to sell. An entrepreneur should be able to answer the majority of a customers' questions without hesitation. If you do not know the answer, be honest with your customers and tell them that you will research it and get back to them in a timely manner. Then, follow up with the customer. This will show that you truly care about their needs.

In addition, profitable entrepreneurs will be savvy about their customers' needs. Rather than try to sell a product to someone, ask customers what they need. Then, you can provide the solution to the customer with your product or service. Listening to customers' needs is especially important in a service-based business because it is easy to tailor the service to their needs. If you truly listen to customers and understand what they need, they will realize that you gave them special attention. Consequently, they will feel relaxed with you and will be more apt to do business with you because you have shown them that you really care about making them happy.

Good entrepreneurs will know about their competition. The more you know about your competition, the easier it will be for you to find a niche market. You will be able to differentiate your product and/or service from your competition. Generally, if you are specialized, you will have an easier time tackling a target market.

An excellent entrepreneur will know about the overall market and world events. For example, home improvement centers keep a close watch on the war in Iraq and terrorism. The increased fear of flying has caused people to spend more on their homes for a couple of reasons. First, people have more money because they are not traveling as much. Secondly, because they are not traveling as often, people want to beautify their home, where they are staying longer. In short, the entrepreneur has to be aware and savvy about their surroundings in the world so that they can provide products and services that are in demand.

Conclusion

If you are friendly, ethical, ambitious, task orientated, and savvy, you will achieve success. Achieving success as an entrepreneur takes a lot of hard work and perseverance. Most entrepreneurs fail numerous times before finding their successful niche in the marketplace. I hope you are successful on your first entrepreneurial venture. However, the odds are against you. But do not be afraid to fail, as you are never really failing. If you learn from your mistakes, with persistence you will achieve success! If you have a new business idea and want help in getting things going or advice on a matter, please feel free to contact me. Even if you have been in business awhile and want a second opinion on a matter, do not hesitate to contact me.

Chapter Ten

Your Mission, Should You Choose to Accept

Presented by Joe Keeley

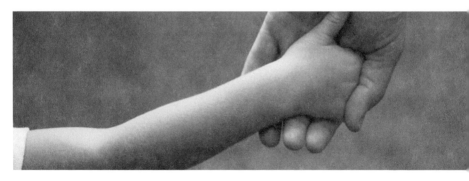

I was sitting in my dorm room, balancing my

checkbook during the end of the spring semester of my freshman year at the University of St. Thomas in St. Paul, Minnesota, when I realized one reoccurring theme: subtraction. It was becoming very evident, as I quickly approached a zero balance, that summer was going to be a welcome change. You see, summer not only meant that the beautiful Minnesota lakes were prime for waterskiing after I had successfully completed my first year of undergraduate studies, but I needed to make some cash. So my search began. I began by listing the possible positions that college students typically hold in any given summer in cities across the United States: pizza delivery driver, waiter, coffee shop barista, and even the prized "intern," which from what I could tell was a glorified, sometimes unpaid, office gopher. There had to be something more, I thought. As a business student eager to land that "dream job" upon graduation, I understood the significance of getting one's "foot in the door," but somehow I figured my landlord would not appreciate my "résumé building experience" when the unpaid internship failed to produce his monthly rent check. And although I thoroughly enjoyed food, I was a bit worried about never being able to remove the pepperoni smell from my car. I was stumped on where to look until one day, staring up at me was a clas-sified ad in the university paper with my summer job. Now, given my upbringing in the small farming community of Grafton, North Dakota and being a college hockey player, I am sure you are thinking the job staring back at me was something very "manly," a job with long hours, one that a college guy could do outside and "feel good about after a honest day's work." Well, in a way you are correct. The ad stated: Nanny Wanted …

I began my first summer as a nanny, or "manny" in my case, with a wonderful family with two boys, ages seven and nine. Although they had a younger sister, my job duties as the family's summer nanny included a multitude of responsibilities primarily centered on being with the boys and organizing their packed schedule. Each sunny Minnesota morning, I arrived around 7:30 a.m. to roust the boys for another day of activities. I wore a plethora of "hats" as a nanny for the family over the three years I worked for them, including hockey coach, cook, referee, disciplinarian, teacher, student, and friend. Little did I realize, however, during my first summer as a nanny that I was not just delaying the inevitable "internship" needed to climb the corporate ladder that I spoke about earlier, but rather I had stumbled upon an opportunity that would provide me with hands-on business experience unmatched by any internship or entry-level job for years to come.

As the summer progressed, and I became more familiar with the families in the neighborhood as well as a staple in the little league car pool, I began to realize that having children involved in activities was no simple task. The boys for whom I was caring and most of the children in the neighborhood were involved in almost every activity under the sun from sports practice to music lessons, as well as added pressure to excel in school. To further complicate matters, I saw more and more families with both parents holding full-time careers piled on top of the responsibility of full-time parenthood. I began to realize that families of today were different than those of even 10 years ago and thus needed a different type of childcare. Traditional daycare centers didn't seem to fully meet the needs of today's families, not to mention the active schedules of the children. Perhaps it's because I am a male and thus do not fit the mold of your typical "nanny," but many parents commented on how great they thought it was having a "guy nanny" be with the boys. I began to see that I was much more than a typical "babysitter," but rather was an "Active Role Model." Parents would often stop me at a swim meet or baseball game and ask if I had any friends who would be interested in working with their children, which ironically I did.

This simple inquiry from a few families prompted me to start a business. I knew plenty of my fellow classmates would make great "nannies," and I knew the families would pay me to connect them for the convenience factor alone. And so I became a business owner. The company, originally known as College Summer Nannies, was incorporated in March of 2001 with very little savings, which I used to cover filing fees and create a few informational folders, forms, and business cards. The original concept was to connect families with outgoing, reliable college students to be nannies for their children during the summer months for a nominal fee. I thought I had it all planned out. I would connect a few families with nannies, make a little cash, put "business owner" on my résumé, and bypass the entire "meaningless" internship process to a good-paying "safe" position in corporate America upon graduation. However (and fortunately I might add), things didn't quite work out that way. Although the company successfully placed 12 nannies in the first year of operations, I never did pay myself that "extra cash" I had been so motivated by. It wasn't long before the business became much more to me than a means to an end. It became a passion.

I remember hearing a former business owner once saying "don't worry about the money, it will come," and thinking he was nuts. It was easy for him to say since he had all the money he could possibly spend. But in retrospect, that is exactly what I did with College Nannies in the very beginning and still do to this day. I began to work on the business for its own sake, and its success became more important than personal financial gain. After all, I was working for free. Now don't get me wrong, I am not suggesting that you ignore the financial component of a business, but I do feel that there needs to be more than money motivating an entrepreneur to take a wild idea that everyone says is crazy and attempt to grow a business out of it. Being an entrepreneur is far too much work and the risks seem to highly outweigh the rewards to be involved for money's sake alone.

It is on this premise of building a business for its own sake that I have operated the company under for the past three years. College Summer Nannies morphed and changed its name to College Nannies as its scope of services widened and improved. The company grew by enjoying rave reviews from satisfied families, nannies, as well as multiple media outlets. And although there always seemed to be a fair share of "fires" that needed immediate extinguishing like most businesses, all decisions seemed to come naturally and stemmed from the company's core values: strengthening families, continuing growth and education, honesty, integrity, and the pursuit of the common good. These values have made the answer to any potentially difficult business decision clear. Such decisions and practices, because of multiple corporate scandals in recent years, seem to be on the forefront of many business-related discussions.

We all meet ethical crossroads almost everyday in both our personal and professional lives without even knowing it. It is our personal values, and thus our company's values (specifically in startup firms), that don't allow the situation to become a dilemma because we intuitively already know the answer. Granted, it should be noted that knowing this answer might not make the decision any easier. You may realize that the right decision to make may not render the best short-term result for the company in terms of cash flow or profits, but hopefully it does increase the chances of creating a sustainable long-term organization, and most importantly, you know it is the right decision. For example, at College Nannies we conduct background screens on each nanny we place on behalf of each hiring family. I suppose it would be possible not to conduct the proper screens on every candidate assuming the screening results would be clear. This would allow the screening costs to fall to the bottom line of the company, which would improve the company's profitability in the short term. However, not screening employees would be inconsistent with the company's values, misleading our clients and ultimately destroying the company's reputation. Theoretically, it is an ethical dilemma, but it is not even a question to consider in my mind. By establishing a strong foundation of values and principles in the company from its inception, I feel many ethical dilemmas are not dilemmas at all. As an entrepreneur, it is one's personal values that are translated into the mission, vision, and culture of the company that he or she not only has the opportunity but obligation to create and foster in the organization. Decisions have and will continue to be made within the College Nannies by asking the question of whether or not the decision at hand promotes the mission of "Making a positive difference in the lives of children, families and nannies alike."

With a solid foundation laid for the company, one hundred or so satisfied clients and graduation looming, I felt I was ready for the "the real world." I was excited to have the opportunity to hopefully realize the full potential of the business now that I was able to devote my all of my efforts to it without the distraction of final examines. Nevertheless, having a business while being a student was a great experience. Being a student carries along with it a safety net of sorts. It seems that everyone in society accepts and embraces students, so anything achieved above and beyond that is looked upon as extraordinary. The lesson to be learned here (for current students) is to be sure to take advantage of your student status, whether it is through starting a business merely for learning purposes or leveraging the fact of being a student entrepreneur to gain publicity for your business. By starting a company while in college, I not only enhanced my classroom education by having a real-life case study to apply to issues and projects in class, but I was also able to, with the help of many, create a company that is valuable and is making a positive difference for families on a daily basis.

Since graduation, the company has again changed its name from College Nannies to College Nannies & Tutors, with the addition of both in-home tutoring and homework help services. We have expanded our business scope and services not only to provide nannies, but also educational tutors for families as what we like to call "Active Role Models for Active Children." The company has changed significantly since the initial concept, but the mission has remained constant. Change is inevitable and vital to business success; however, I believe it is important for entrepreneurs to stay true to their roots, values, and personal mission for their own lives to ensure the integrity of themselves, regardless of the ventures they become involved in. The company still holds and will continue to hold the same values, principles, and mission that were developed early on when it was just me, mentoring two boys as their summer nanny.

Chapter Eleven

Visual Moments Frozen in Time

Presented by Matt Staver

There has never been a day in my life where photography didn't play a part. Some aspect of freezing visual moments
of time has been and will continue to be an influential and guiding
force in my life.

Early on, photography was the form of my family's income. It determined our lifestyle and where my dad would be the next day. He
traveled around the world making amazing photographs and amassing
wonderful experiences.

In high school, I borrowed a camera. That marked the first time I
began directing how photography would affect my life. It was during
those first years of working hard (for the yearbook), skipping classes
(to take pictures for the yearbook), and taking as much advice from
my dad (about pictures that were for the yearbook) as I could stand
that I realized what I wanted to do for the rest of my life. At about
14 years of age, I knew I was a photographer. Seeing my own credit
line and watching others look at my photographs proved to be a very
rewarding experience.

Then, it was time for college; I applied to Colorado State University
only as it boasted the best daily student-run newspaper, The Collegian,
of the in-state schools. Since it provided the best opportunity, I knew
I would do whatever it took to get there.

One of the major obstacles of young entrepreneurship surfaced when
I applied to work as a photographer at The Collegian. (Wahoo! I was
finally going to get paid for taking pictures.) This obstacle wasn't sub-
tle about surfacing either; it flew from the water like an 800 pound

Marlin threatening to snap the line connecting me and my goal.
They told me I was too young to work there. They said I didn't have
enough experience and probably wasn't mature enough for the
responsibilities the job entailed. Being considered too young and/or
inexperienced has been (and will be for many young entrepreneurs) a
major hurdle to overcome. It appears over and over again.

I needed to prove to them I could do it. It never occurred to me to
just wait a year or two and apply again when I was "old enough."
They were worried I would not bring back a photograph good
enough to be in the paper, leaving them literally with a hole to fill.
With a little courage, enough confidence, and intrinsic motivation, I
devised a plan that would benefit them, pose very little risk, and
would show them that I could do the job. I pitched the plan to the
photo editor: I would work for free for two weeks, going on the same
assignments as current staff photographers, allowing him to judge the
quality of my work, and The Collegian wouldn't incur any additional
costs. With nothing to lose, the editor soon sent me on my first
assignment.

Luck showed up when there was an assignment turned in that none
of the other photographers could make. I was unenthusiastically
assigned to shoot it alone. The film came back, the pictures lived up
to the standards of the paper, and not only was I offered a permanent
position, but they paid me for this one and all future assignments.
To overcome the "too young/inexperienced" hurdle of entrepreneurship, I adopted a combination of:
· People skills: convincing others to hear your plan;
· Knowledge of others' fears: formulating a low-risk plan that

demonstrates that you do what you say you can do;

· Ability: being able to execute the plan and actually do what you say you can do;

This plan allowed me and will also permit you to clear that hurdle, maybe not as easily as an Olympic track star, but it should get you over the bar.

Working for The Collegian was great experience, but soon I wanted to grow. Not knowing the steps necessary to expand as a photographer, I called on my dad, an expert in the field who was not a direct competitor. Suddenly, I became very self-conscious. I didn't want to rely on anyone for help, especially my dad. I wanted to be successful on my own. If I used his tips, advice, or contacts (or anyone else's for that matter) to grow and advance-well, it just didn't feel right -- at first.

But I swallowed my pride, took the advice, used the contacts, and got my foot in the door at The Denver Post, the biggest newspaper in Colorado. They didn't give me assignments right away because I was "too young" and "too inexperienced" to produce the quality of work they demanded in such a reputable publication. But, like before, I used the low-risk plan to show them I could perform to their standards. I would periodically send in photos for the photo editors to look at with the intention of getting published as a stand-alone feature. I also made myself available for last-minute assignments no one else could cover. This forced me to skip some classes, helping speed my learning of time management and priorities. After all, a legitimate reason to occasionally skip Basic Accounting was definitely a perk of the job.

Over a relatively short period of time, I began getting regular assignments from The Denver Post. They paid about six times more than The Collegian, provided a huge jump in prestige, and forced me to grow as a photographer.

For a long time, I had known about digital manipulation of photographs. I enjoyed taking pictures of my friends and family and making them have a huge head, or digitally pasting their head on the picture of someone else's body. But it was when I began working for The Denver Post that I realized the possible implications of digital manipulation of photographs. They never saw my film. I scanned the negative (a year or so after I began working for them, digital cameras were used, and they offered the same potential problems) and emailed the photograph to them. I was a young photographer, still learning the trade. Sure, I missed some important moments, maybe cutting off a football player's arm; theoretically it was possible to "fix" these mistakes digitally. However, I knew manipulating a photograph poses serious problems. I even wrote a paper about digital manipulation of photographs for my freshman composition class. My belief was then, as it is now, that the word "photograph" refers to freezing a visual moment in time. A photograph shows reality. The opening paragraph of that freshman paper describes how I felt: "Digital manipulation of photographs can be a valuable part of photography when the viewer is informed about the changes or if the changes don't alter the reality in the photograph. Digital manipulation of a photograph that alters its content and changes its reality should, however, require that the new image no longer be called a photograph because it can harm people and trick the viewer."

There were times when I could have "fixed" a picture to make it better.

I remember joking with the editors at The Collegian about a basketball photograph where the ball was just above the top edge of the picture. I told them I would have paid $500 for the ball to be just a little bit lower. But not only would that go against my personal beliefs and against my responsibility as an editorial photographer, it could and probably would come back to haunt me. I would lose credibility as a photojournalist. People would question every picture I had ever taken or would take in the future. "Did he actually take that picture, or did he create it on the computer?" viewers would ask. I would not be able to get work as a photographer for a long, long time.

So, from early on, I decided what a photograph was to me. I decided that the short-term benefits of altering the content of a photograph paled to the long-term consequences. It was more than just a decision; it turned into a core belief, something that helped define who I am as a person and how I do business. Given the potential disaster of only considering the short-term outcome of a decision, it seems sensible to look down the road.

Things continued to go well. Matthew Staver Photography began gaining new clients and name recognition while I kept improving my photography skills. With all this new responsibility and workload, some things that seemed like trivial details slipped through the cracks. One evening, my car was broken into and the majority of my camera equipment stolen. Apparently I had let the camera insurance lapse a few months ago, and neither renters nor auto insurance would cover it. This was a pivotal moment for the future of Matthew Staver Photography. I was upset. I was mad. I was confused. Could this be a sign? I thought, maybe it's time to quit struggling to gain new clients, quit struggling to keep current clients happy. Maybe it's time to stop being the secretary, accountant, bill collector, director of marketing, CEO, and the photographer. Maybe it is time to relax, go with the flow, and apply for a normal job with a salary, vacation, and benefits. It was definitely time for some serious thinking. Basically I had three options:

· Buy all new gear and continue with Matthew Staver Photography
· Start another venture
· Get a "normal" job

It was all I could think about for a full week. My thinking began pushing me toward getting a normal job and taking pictures on the side because I still enjoyed photography. Life would be easier; I would have more money, maybe lease a new car, and I would get a paid vacation! By the end of that week, I was pretty sure what to do: get a normal job. But once I had made that decision, something inside me told me if I did, I would never be satisfied. It was around that time that I began to question my and society's definition of success. I was intrinsically compelled to be a freelance photographer, to freeze visual moments of time.

Therefore, I bought new cameras, new lenses, new batteries, and new flashes. Matthew Staver Photography even invested in a new top-of-the-line digital camera.

Things got rolling with the help of some good luck, encouragement from friends and family, and more determination. For example, I won the North American Collegiate Entrepreneur Award (renamed the Global Student Entrepreneur Awards) for my region. Some of the prize money helped ease a bit of the burden of buying the new equipment. And, it freed up enough cash to buy a plane ticket to Bangkok. Above all else I was a photographer; I wanted to see some amazing things. I wanted to photograph monks living in a temple in Thailand. My bags were packed: one extra pair of pants, one extra shirt, some socks and underwear, and camera gear. It was only a three-week trip; how bad could a shirt smell? And off I flew to what fortified my decision to keep working on making Matthew Staver Photography a viable business.

The monks yielded intimate photographs and the opportunity to grow as a photographer. I learned to see light in different ways. Through several late nights of sitting around the fire inside the temple grounds talking with my new monk friends, I learned more about success and began formulating my own definition.

The next few years literally flew by while I worked to gain new clients, work for current clients, and graduate from college. I took photo trips to Italy, Japan, Holland, and Cuba and began working on an inspirational photo book project. During this time, I began further refining my version of the definition of success. It's not finished (hey, I'm still learning), but to me, success isn't only a large salary, a new BMW, and never having to ask for advice. Instead, it's doing exactly what you do every day, even if you've won the lottery. It's being able to accept advice and not be ashamed that you're not entirely self-sufficient. It's being able to offer honest answers when people ask for advice and selflessly giving back to the community. Success is not feeling guilty or suffering consequences when you go for a run at 3 p.m. on a warm afternoon.

OK, now about that luck factor to which I have alluded: Good Luck. There certainly is an element of chance involved in luck -- things that a person cannot control. However, luck isn't entirely chance. A person can put him- or herself in the position for good luck, and I believe individuals make a large portion of their own luck. It was lucky that no other photographer at The Collegian could take that first assignment, but if I weren't there, and if I didn't have my camera with me and didn't want to work before school started, there would have been no luck. Yes, I was lucky to win the GSEA contest; someone else could have entered with a better business plan, and my teacher didn't have to tell me about it. But if I didn't enter, if I didn't have a viable business, the luck wouldn't have occurred. So look for luck, get into position for good luck, and things will start falling into place.

Finally, take advantage of every opportunity presented to you. (That being said, when YOUR company needs photographs for advertising, its annual report, or any other purpose, you know who to call!) Eagerly accept help from family members, monks, and luck. Don't be afraid to rearrange your definition of success, and don't forget that some risks are worth taking. Not many people win the lottery, but that doesn't prevent you from truly enjoying life.

Chapter Twelve

Cowboy Ethics

Presented by Miles Mays

Growing up on a cattle ranch in central

Washington State, my brothers and I had a vast playground for adventure. Yet what was fun to a young whippersnapper soon became a challenging juggling act between academics, athletics, and my duties on our ranch. My plethora of activities taught me discipline, organization, and a strong work ethic. Because of my thirst for knowledge and my desire for a challenge, I attended a private school to pursue a degree in engineering. I am now in my senior year at Gonzaga University in Spokane, Washington, majoring in civil engineering. Eventually, I plan to attend graduate school to obtain a master's degree in hydraulic engineering. On weekends and holidays, I often travel home to oversee my business and help my family with work on the ranch.

My entrepreneurial spirit emerged during winter vacation of my high school sophomore year. It snowed day after day, leaving three to four feet piled on the ground. It was the greatest amount of snowfall central Washington had experienced in many years. Most saw this as an inconvenience to their everyday activities; however, I saw the snow as an opportunity. A strapping young lad of 16 years, I had youth and determination on my side. Beaming with confidence, my older brother Marcus and I decided we would grab our snow shovels and go door-to-door in residential neighborhoods and offer our services shoveling roofs. The morning hours slipped away, the afternoon soon passed, and we had only received one job. Our great idea was seemingly a bust.

The next day dawned, and roofs throughout the Kittitas Valley started to collapse under the weight of the snow as the weather was warming.

That night, the local newspaper displayed pictures of collapsed barns, garages, and houses.

The following morning, opportunity struck. The people who had turned us down just days before were now wishing they had our services. We were inundated with phone calls from concerned homeowners and business owners who wanted their roofs cleared of snow. Acting fast, we recruited five fellow high school wrestlers to help us with our newfound niche. At home, our mother answered the incessantly ringing phone, recorded job orders, and became our designated dispatcher. Our crew spread out across the valley, trying to meet everyone's needs and requests as we worked from daybreak until 10 or 11 at night. We were never sure what to charge our customers for our services, but we tried to be consistent and fair to everyone. Nevertheless, we gave special consideration to people in need who weren't capable of paying our typical rate.

Christmas break passed, and we had spent the majority of it on rooftops, shoveling our hearts out. Never had I been so glad to go back to school, and as consolation to soothe my aching muscles, I had a couple thousand dollars in my pocket. As a 16-year-old sophomore, I had earned an impressive salary in my own business enterprise. My brother and I had seen a niche and capitalized on an opportunity.

Our small-scale snow-shoveling venture had made a substantial profit with little investment because we were willing to place our lives at some degree of risk by climbing on rooftops when no one else was willing. As every entrepreneur will confess, we worked far beyond the concept of an "eight-to-five" workday. Additionally, I had discovered how to choose workers with a similar work ethic, how to delegate responsibilities, and how to share profits with these employees while still earning a respectable profit. This experience led me to my next venture: a cattle truck washout. But first, allow me to explain the evolution of my business.

I grew up in the Kittitas Valley in Central Washington. The valley is scattered mostly with hay farms and small-scale cattle ranches. However, the cattle market through the mid 1980s to the mid 1990s was far from lucrative. Many of the local ranchers had to downsize their businesses, decreasing their inventory of cattle, and many went bankrupt. Others simply subdivided their land for development. However, my father was able to stick with it, selling none of our land and keeping our family livestock business afloat. In 1994, opportunity struck via a contact my father had established as a result of his commitment to the beef industry. He was asked if he was willing to expand his business overseas, by receiving shipments of cattle from Hawaii. My father saw this as a great opportunity to diversify his existing business and accepted the challenge.

The origin and progression of the cattle business in Hawaii is rather interesting. However, to understand the nature of the beef industry in Hawaii as it is today, it is necessary to take a step back in history. From the 16th to the 19th century, the whaling industry was very lucrative as whale blubber was used extensively in soap-making and as a source of fuel. The whaling ships touring the Pacific Ocean would port in Hawaii to replenish food and supplies. Before the days of refrigeration, stocking a ship with an adequate supply of meat was a challenge. Opportunity struck the ranchers and landowners in the area. By raising beef on the islands and salting the meat for preservation, they could supply the ships with the food necessary to feed their crews. Thus, the cattle industry was born to the islands.

When refrigeration became possible, there was no longer a need to buy beef from the Hawaiian ranchers. Rather, the ships would stock up their supplies on the mainland for their expeditions. As a result, the number of cattle in Hawaii began to grow exponentially. The supply of beef greatly exceeded the demand, and Hawaiian ranchers were faced with the dilemma of how to market their beef. Their resolution was to ship the majority of their cattle to the mainland, where they could be finished to slaughter-weight cost efficiently, and where there was both a greater demand for their product and a better market. Today, there are neither commercial feedlots nor slaughterhouses in Hawaii. Currently 80% of Hawaiian cattle are shipped to North America.

In 1994, seeing an opportunity to expand our family's livestock business, the Crooked Arrow Ranch became a receiving station for shipments of yearling cattle overseas from Hawaii. Upon arrival at the port of Tacoma, the containers full of cattle were placed on trucks and hauled to our ranch in Ellensburg, Washington. After unloading, the cattle containers needed to be washed out before being shipped back to Hawaii, clean and refilled with feed. This need was the birth of Flying M Washout, a new venture for my brothers and me. We were challenged to design a truck washout system that was both efficient and profitable.

In 1996, the initial year of business, the washout used one trash pump to wash out 54 containers. My brother and I purchased the trash pump along with the fire hoses. Our washout arrangement was rather rudimentary. The trucks simply backed up to an irrigation ditch on a slight decline, and we fed the hoses into the trucks and began washing. However, by 1999, the number of containers increased to more than 100, and more employees were hired on shipment days to help wash out. Again, these employees were fellow high-school athletes who were willing to work on the weekends to make a considerable amount of money in a short amount of time. In addition to hiring more employees to meet the increased demand, the washout was completely renovated. The new washout used a more complex wastewater drainage system and a top-of-the-line pumping schema. A concrete drainage structure was constructed consisting of an 18-inch slotted culvert that transports the wastewater into an irrigation ditch. From that point, the wastewater is distributed over our grazing pastures. Our view of ranching is a holistic one; we saw the potential of using a natural fertilizer -- namely manure -- to fertilize our grazing pastures. Because we use no chemical sprays or fertilizers in our pasture management plan, the diluted manure is used as a natural fertilizer and is an asset to our operations.

My continuing education in dynamic fluid mechanics and water resource management has been critical to the technicalities and improvements of the washout system. The washout business my brother and I started and expanded opened my eyes to other opportunities. Perhaps the most valuable result of this venture was that it gave me confidence to make my own decisions about what to do with my time and money. Because of my experiences with Flying M Washout, combined with my college educational experiences, I have

learned a great deal about owning and operating a small business.
I collaborated with my brothers and parents on my next venture as an
entrepreneur. Profits from Flying M Washout allowed my brother
and me to expand our business to the livestock sector in 2001, creating
Flying M Livestock. We purchased 88 bred cows. It was a "spur of
the moment" decision to buy this herd. Our uncle was selling out of
the cow/calf business, and his herd was solid and healthy. Although it
consisted mostly of older cows, they were proven mothers and were
accustomed to the environment in the valley. We decided to take a
risk and try our hand in the cow/calf business.

Our cows calve on our ranch between February and May. When the
calves are several weeks old, the pairs are hauled to the mountains
where we continue to feed them hay until the grass is ready for grazing
-- usually in the first week of April. They remain in the mountains,
being rotated through pastures, until September. In the fall, the herd
returns to graze on irrigated valley pastures until the snow covers the
ground. The calves are weaned from their mothers in late fall. When
winter arrives, winter feeding begins, and we look forward to the
first calf. The annual cycle begins again.

Recently, the cowherd has increased in quantity, but more significantly,
quality. Flying M Livestock now owns 240 head of Black Angus
mother cows, which are bred to Black Angus and Wagu bulls. The
Wagu bulls, when bred to Angus cows, produce a small but strong
calf. Because the calves are considerably smaller than if they were
bred to Angus bulls, labor is much easier on the cows. As a standard
practice, we breed our first-calf heifers to Wagu Bulls, so that their
first birth is as smooth as possible. Additionally, the Wagu-bred calves

bring a premium price. Wagu-bred beef is highly regarded and in great demand. Recently, Flying M Livestock formed an LLC with each member owning one-quarter interest in the company. Certainly, Flying M Livestock has and will continue to develop and expand.

In addition to our cowherd and washout business, my brother and I recently pursued a different undertaking. During the summer of 2003, while I was interning with an engineering firm, my brother and I made an investment in a herd of steers. An opportunity arose to furnish cattle to a man living north of Seattle (about 100 miles from our home ranch) who participated in cattle cutting, which is a recreational spin-off of traditional ranching practices. This particular cow-cutter wanted a herd of approximately 40 steers for the summer months of June, July, and August to use for practice and horse training. However, he did not want to buy the herd; rather, he wanted to lease the cattle from someone to reduce his investment risk. He agreed to feed the steers for the summer at no cost to my brother and me, and additionally he volunteered to pay all freight costs to and from Seattle.

At that time the cattle market was strong and we gambled that it would hold through August, estimating the cattle would gain at least one pound per day at no cost to us. As we predicted, the market stayed strong throughout the summer and the cattle averaged a gain of approximately one hundred pounds. Our 38 steers were then sold, and we earned a considerable profit from our investment. By taking a risk based on our assumption, we had made a substantial profit. Although some luck was involved, we considered the venture to be a calculated risk.

In addition to being a profitable venture, my involvement in the live-stock industry has been a satisfying endeavor. I enjoy my cattleman's life and plan to continue it as a sideline to my engineering profession. The experiences and challenges of growing up in the ranching business have taught me that to succeed I need to work hard, remain creative and flexible, and always be open to new ideas and opportunities. I plan on applying the foundation of principles that I have established in the livestock industry to my future as I pursue a career in engineering. Perhaps the thing I love most about engineering are the challenges faced. Such challenges require scientific thinking, but even more importantly, practical, creative thinking in order to formulate the optimal solution.

In my younger years, I did not have a profound grasp on the concept of formalized "business ethics." Rather, I followed my gut feeling and what my heart told me. Basically, my approach to ethics was to "do what I know is right." Today, six years later, as a senior at a Jesuit University, I have had my share of ethics courses. However, in light of these courses taught by professors and Jesuits with doctorates in philosophy and ethics, I still take my own approach to ethics. I call my approach to the moral code "cowboy ethics." It consists simply of "do what feels right, what your heart and your gut tell you to do." However, there are a few necessities that make this approach effective. First of all, your heart and your gut must be properly constructed with strong beliefs about matters of principle. These beliefs mark the framework with which your decisions are made.

Personally, the values that form my foundation of principles have mostly been constructed from my parents' approach to business.

Some of these values include, but are not limited to, honesty, integrity, competency, reliability, and the ability to be forward-looking and inspiring among your constituents. My parents have always worked for themselves, much like other typical entrepreneurs. Success has not been easily achieved by the family livestock business, but by remaining consistent with their ethical approach, they have become very successful entrepreneurs, financially, ethically, and emotionally. Raised in an entrepreneurial setting, I experienced firsthand the dilemmas that many entrepreneurs face. Thankfully, my father always made morally and ethically correct decisions. For this reason, he is one the most well-respected men in the cattle industry. Never has a customer or client of my father been cheated or lied to in any way; my father always "tells it how it is." Witnessing his trials and tribulations has been paramount for me as a young entrepreneur, as I strive to become as well respected as he is. As a result, to "do what my heart and my gut tell me to do" is paralleling the perceived actions of my father in the same situation.

Certainly, there were many challenges that I faced along the way in my business endeavors, none of which caused me to give up. By remaining open to new ideas, advice, and being stubborn about my ability to succeed, I overcame adversity in several instances. One great thing about being young is that you have almost nothing to lose when you venture out and take a risk in the business world. Certainly, you are better off failing when you are my age and have nothing to lose versus when you are older and have a family, a mortgage, and a career. As a young entrepreneur, I have learned to look forward to the future and the challenges that it will bring.

With respect to cowboy ethics and what I call the cowboy mindset, there is one concept that drives my everyday approach to life: "If you're not getting better, you're getting worse, because nobody stays the same." This principle applies to everything: business, learning, academics, and even your everyday health. I personally strive to make the most out of every minute of my life. If whatever I am currently doing is not something that will make me a better person in some way, then I will pursue a different task that will.

Unquestionably, this single principle of cowboy ethics is something that every person of every faith can embrace. For me, it has lead to a more successful, productive, and optimistic lifestyle.

Chapter Thirteen

Peace Begins with Children

Presented by Narcedalia Lozano

When I was six years old, I had so many problems at school because I could not write very well. I messed up letters, and had difficulty concentrating on my classes. My mother took me to a wonderful doctor whose diagnosis was hyperactivity or "a problem of direction." She suggested I should be introduced to music lessons in order to improve my learning skills and concentration. As I began to play the flute and sing once a week, my grades did improve. At that time, and in spite of all my problems in writing, my parents always talked positively toward me and gave me encouragement to set goals and accomplish them. They always said, "Sooner or later, the people who make a big effort will get the rewards they deserve."Thanks to both influences, I went from being a terrible student to a great student, graduating with honors, and becoming a caring person about the community.

Even though I lived in a world of loving parents and equality of opportunity, I was certainly aware of the existence of people less fortunate than me. It always hurt me a lot to watch children as victims of war, people in poverty, and orphaned, abandoned, and abused children, without the love and security they needed to develop in a healthy way. I cried at night about the conditions of these people, especially the children. It embarrassed me to do so, but I felt I could not do anything else about it. Thinking about my own life -- so full of love and opportunities -- I felt miserable that I could not share everything with them. At just 20 years of age, I had already traveled around the globe, learned so many things, and participated in several congresses, symposiums, and seminars with young people of different nationalities who listened to social activists, world leaders, and Nobel Peace Prize winners. I had lived with and talked to people of every religion, race, culture, and socioeconomic background. At the same age, I was often recognized as a leader as well, but that meant nothing to me. I had also won some prizes by then, but all of them made me feel more miserable and without a sense of direction. I felt I was called to do big things because all the gifts and talents I was graced with should be put at the service of the ones who need them the most.

While I was studying my major in International Relations at the Monterrey Institute of Technology (ITESM), I went to the International Symposium for Mediation and Conflict Resolution in Holland and Belgium. There were many speakers there; some of them impressed me because they believed in the theory of deterrence, which means that every country should do their best to recruit their armies and accumulate weapons in order to dissuade and discourage other countries from threatening and attacking them. For example, if one country attacks another, the result would be devastation for both countries and maybe for the whole world. This destruction greatly frightened me. I realized that there will always be countries less powerful than the others; there will always be people with less opportunities and economic possibilities than the rest of them. I wondered what I could do to help. I definitely believed that fear should not be the only way to avoid war.

I continued to listen to other speakers who said that war was inevitable and a natural process humanity should face. Others said war should be prevented because once it breaks out, it is a very costly and difficult process to stop. There was a video of many people in the African Continent who were making theater presentations in order to remember the Hutus and Tutsis conflict. At the end of the presentation, all actors shouted "Forgive but not forget!" Everybody in the auditorium, from every country and every race who attended the symposium, was crying at the sight of people trying to alleviate through art the sufferings of watching their families being murdered, raped, and abused. They were trying to recover and start their lives over again, to restore their hope. I realized art can make people bring out all their feelings and find themselves, forgive, and continue living their lives. I asked myself, is it possible to prevent war? I did not know, but I tried to do something that seemed a desperate impulse to give something back to the most vulnerable group: the children.

I suddenly remembered perfectly my first music lesson, my music instructor's words, and all that I learned in my classes. I decided to go to the nearest orphanage and began a music workshop with 40 children from five to six years old. I did just that, going two hours a week on Saturdays. It turned out to be one of the greatest experiences of my life. I remembered myself in the music lessons, my face looking around the classroom, at my fellow students, and up at my teacher. I also remember the music concert that was organized at the end of the semester, in which I and the other students could show in a theater what we had learned. Of course, it was very satisfactory to see my parents in the audience applauding my effort!

I enjoyed the experience of sharing things I liked very much and that had turned every aspect of my life in a richer experience. Since 2000, I have continued going to Casa Paterna La Gran Familia orphanage. The children advanced a lot, so I decided to organize a music concert. I invited the community to watch these children's musical achievements. I noticed how, in just one semester of music lessons, these children for the first time had made a quantum leap in their lives, their expectations, their goals, and their self-esteem. They experienced the challenge to show themselves and a group of people their accomplishments. Their faces became illuminated, their goals grew, and they were able to see a world of opportunities opening in front of their faces. The vicious cycle of poverty and indifference was evolving into a virtuous cycle of peace and prosperity.

After the concert, many people became interested in sharing their abilities, talents, and values with those children. Many of them were afraid because did not feel they could have the capacity to teach what they know since they were not "experts." After sharing their talents, they become confident and participated even more. Since 2000, 1,174 volunteers and social service students have conducted workshops in music (piano, recorder, guitar, singing, percussion, and violin), dance (ballet, folk, jazz, and contemporary), theatre, pastry-making, the history of Mexico, didactic mathematics, chemistry, physics, painting, drawing, creative children's literature, soccer, Taekwondo, Kung-fu, karate, declamation, oratory, choral poetry, languages (English, French, Japanese), and values to children of Casa Paterna La Gran Familia, DIF Capullos, Casa Hogar el Refugio de Monterrey, Villa Eudes, Ministerios de Amor, Bethel, Estancia Temporal del DIF. We have reached around 3,400 children. Every semester, the children show the fruits of their efforts in the art, science, and sports workshops through a Concierto por la Paz that is performed in a local auditorium with an enthusiastic audience. Today, we recruit university students from ITESM, UDEM, and UR, and offer community social service hours for teaching the workshops in their interest areas. Students from other universities such as UANL, Arte AC, CEDIM,

Universidad del Noreste, and graduates also participate as volunteers. Today, we are expanding this effort to other states in Mexico, and we plan to grow and reach all Mexican and Latin American children. I realized I had stopped crying for the images I saw on TV or on the newspapers about abused children in poor situations. Instead of crying, I made life to work for them, to make it possible for them to see a bright future, to give them the opportunity to be good citizens, and to motivate them to grow.

In 2002, I found a social enterprise named Fundacion La Paz Comienza con los Niños, or Peace Begins with Children Foundation. Its mission is to create a culture of peace and prosperity among children through art, science, and sports. I registered the name legally and secured funding. This program works because it makes a positive impact on children because they can learn something useful for their lives. Volunteers have found a way to share what they love to do with their children who do not have access to these kinds of workshops. The volunteers experience a change because we all get more out of giving than receiving. Many times, we have taken over 1,200 children to an auditorium to attend professional performances, such as the ITESM Chamber Orchestra, so they can learn every musical instrument and their sounds. The children have also enjoyed theater, such as Shakespeare's plays, and shows like folk dances from different countries. With these experiences, they become motivated to improve their efforts in their workshops because they look up to professionals in order to follow a good role model.

After studying one semester at Harvard University, I made an investigation about the work of UNICEF in order to attain poverty reduction through education and health services. One subject that caught my attention was Education for Peace. "What is that?" I asked myself. It sounds beautiful, but could it be possible to educate for peace in order to prevent conflict? I only read a few words about this program, but I nevertheless wanted to apply this concept to the workshops. I wanted the volunteers to design their workshops and introduce certain values to promote a culture of peace such as respect, truth, fraternity, perseverance, peace, love, teamwork, honesty, freedom, and goal-setting.

Through creativity, we teach these values to children. Every semester a Concierto por la Paz is presented, and each time more people attend this event and applaud the children's effort. Many enterprises have shared economical resources with our foundation to buy musical instruments, sports equipment, and other supplies for the children. Grupo Galeria, HEB, Price Waterhouse Cooper, Carl's Jr., and, of course, many people have helped with their time, counseling, and money to the foundation. All of the children who participate in the workshops are given the necessary materials to develop properly in their classes. It does not matter if it is a musical instrument such as a recorder, guitar, percussion, brass instrument, or keyboard; or if it is a pair of dance shoes, painting tools, martial arts suits and equipment, or literature books.

The hardest thing about my line of work is directing the donated money not to what the foundation needs, but to what the donor intended the funding for. If in our meeting with a company, I brought to the table the necessity of musical instruments and the money was donated, I should accept, despite the many other needs, and especially if I made a compromise with the donor that "this money would be for this," to buy what the donor requested, not what are the priorities for our foundation.

Although so many people would like to work for this kind of foundation, it is important to choose the right people whose values and goals are compatible with the organization's mission. There are those who look for a job where they can earn lots of money; for them, the company's mission or products don't matter. Nevertheless, it is my responsibility to look always for staff who are interested because they feel the vision and goals of our civil organization is related to their values and principles.

The process of constituting a business or a civil organization in Mexico is a little complicated, but it is important to work hard and endure. I have often closed my ears to many people who told me "You are crazy! Children will not get out of their situation; they will be like their parents. It is impossible to break those patterns! That what you do is impossible; it cannot be done!" "A civil organization is only for rich people who do not need to work." "To get the permission to give deductibles will be almost impossible." "You are too young to do this kind of thing. Enjoy your life and do not think about others." There have been many comments to discourage me, but closing my ears and my eyes to those people was important in order to advance. One must believe that there are not impossible dreams; one must believe everything is possible and that limitations are only in our mind, and those are most of the time created by ourselves because we are afraid of failure. One must believe there is nothing to lose in order to take risks and attain our goals.

Today, I am developing an enterprise that will teach children the most advanced learning techniques. I hope to make this enterprise grow so that I can secure more funds for my civil organization to get more children into the virtuous cycle of peace and prosperity.

Chapter Fourteen

The Road Ahead

Presented by William Barrett

I love owning a business; it is the most rewarding

thing I have ever done. I wake up excited about what the day will bring and look forward to the possibilities that await me. Owning a business allows me use my talents and abilities to live out and achieve my dreams. Most people would say that entrepreneurs are workaholics. The truth is that entrepreneurs never work. Sure, we spend all of our time in the company doing different tasks. But we do not work. Work is what you do for "the man." With hard work and dedication, you too can live your dream!

Everybody has a different definition of success because of his or her different goals and desires. I believe success is not one moment in time. Success is not prestigious awards or a million dollars in your bank account. Success is not first place based on shortcuts, but rather it is the hard-earned second place. Success is not the easy money but the hard-earned dollar.

Success is a long term journey; it is a lifestyle. It is a path paved with mistakes and failures. Success is getting lost from the trail and admitting to your followers that you are lost and yet having the strength and moral compass to guide them. Success is sacrificing your potential to help someone in need. A successful lifestyle is never easy. It is everybody's goal to be successful. Just like everybody else, I want to be at the top and enjoy the fruits of my labor. But there is something to be said about how you get there. How did you get to the top? How is your rise to money and power marked?

It is important to lead your company in an ethical fashion. Most ethical questions are between what we want to do and what we should do.

The Road Ahead   William Barrett

Everybody has a "little man" named Mr. Conscience who lives inside our head. And it seems as if Mr. Conscience talks to us at the most unwanted times. And what makes it worse is that Mr. Conscience never tells us what we want to hear. For example, I was once in a situation where I was providing cleaning services for an account. It was 3:00 a.m., and I had been working for 20 hours. I was a walking zombie. All I wanted to do was to go home and crawl into bed. The job had to be finished by 7:00 a.m., so I could not come back tomorrow to finish it. The problem was that I still had to vacuum some rooms upstairs. It was in my contract to do this, but I was so tired. My customer would not even notice, I told myself. Then, the little man started talking. I really was not in the mood for the unwanted opinion. Mr. Conscience kept telling me to get out the vacuum and finish the job. I went upstairs and spent the next hour vacuuming. Customers expect you to do what you say you are going to do. This is how you earn their respect.

Being a young entrepreneur gives you some unique advantages. I have found that most people are really supportive. College professors are a great source for information. The professors at my college have an enormous amount of business experience, and they love to help any budding business owners. For instance, I had some problems filing my taxes one year, and I went to one of the teachers to ask for help. She was more than willing to lend me a hand. She helped me decide which expenses to deduct. Her assistance was greatly appreciated.

However, sometimes people look at ambition as a negative thing and will try to derail your success. Some people who have had to take 20 years to get into their position of power are not receptive to those who try to reach that level at a younger age. There is resentment toward young ambition sometimes. Once, I was placing a bid on a cleaning contract. I had a meeting with the individual in charge. The meeting was important to me, so I dressed up in a suit and tie and had my presentation organized. When I got to his office, I noticed his eyes stare at me as I walked in. He was dressed in coveralls. You could tell he was thinking, "Just who in the heck do you think you are?" At that moment, we were on two different levels. I did everything I could to meet this man eye to eye and get some type of commonality between us, but it was no use. He was threatened by my age, and this age was emphasized by my professional attire. The situation got worse when we were discussing how the job should be done. I was respectful, but our opinions were different. Needless to say, I did not get that account. Those situations will inevitably arise, yet it is important not to let them get you down.

The biggest problem with being a young entrepreneur is lack of credibility. I was halfway through a contract when I started crunching numbers to see how much I had already paid out in payroll. The bid went for $2,000, and I had already paid close to that. I soon realized I was losing money. I could have pulled out of the job and gone home, but I had an obligation to my customers. That contract cost me an extra $2,000, but my loss had a silver lining. I proved to the customer that I was serious about business and that I was in it for the long haul. You must prove to your customers that you are credible. Do what you say you are going to do. Let them see the passion you have for your business. When you talk with your clients, let them know how important your business is to you and how important their support is to you. Make them aware of your mission, values, and goals. Tell them that you are aware that young people traditionally are irresponsible, but you are going to prove them wrong. Then do what you say!

It can be frustrating hearing the words "I do not think you are ready for that." One of my clients once said that to me. I was placing a bid for cleanup after a local car race. It was a bigger event than I had ever done before; however, it was well within my ability. When I went to my boss to see if I had gotten the bid, they broke the news to me. I was devastated. My price was reasonable, but they thought I was not ready to take on that extra responsibility. I looked at my boss and said, "What do I have to do to prove to you that I can do the job?" He said he admired my spirit and told me to keep at it, and I would get the account. I did not get the account that year, but when the next year came around, I got the job.

To be successful in business takes perseverance and determination. There will be roadblocks in the way, but it is how you handle those situations that determine your success. For instance, when I decided that I wanted to build a house, I knew it was going to be difficult. The hardest part was convincing a bank to loan me $100,000. I was young and even though I had owned, remodeled, and sold a previous house, the bank was hesitant. Building a house was a big step for me. There was a lot at risk. It took some convincing, but I think it was the fact that I had earned their respect as a businessman that played a major role.

When selecting a business as a young entrepreneur, you might want to select a business with fewer barriers to entry. This means fewer obstacles or requirements to enter that line of business. Do this because you probably do not have a lot of money or skills developed at this point. My first business was a pressure-washing business. I went to Lowe's and bought a pressure washer; then I went home and printed business cards on my ink jet printer. I was in business. In these kinds of businesses, there is enormous competition, so it is important to find a niche. As your business grows, use the money earned and skills acquired to develop specialization in your industry. Always use your youthful vigor as an advantage, and do not ever forget to listen to that little man who lives inside your head.

Our Mission:

To inspire students to adopt entrepreneurial endeavors by
bringing global visibility to undergraduate business owners
whose companies adhere to high ethical standards,
are innovative, profitable, and socially responsible

Our Vision:

To the THE most prestigious honor for
the undergraduate business owner.

The Global Student Entrepreneur[SM] Awards honors undergraduates
who are successful at balancing classes and cash flow, pop quizzes and
payroll, finals and financial statements. Finalists must produce more
than just a financially successful business. A distinguished panel of
judges evaluates their company's quality, service, adaptation to
change, and social impact. The main characters in this book (all
finalists) are a diverse lot of students from various backgrounds and
cultures. The plots are varied and the action is fraught with
obstacles, perseverance, and triumphs.

If you wish to apply for the award or obtain further information,
please visit our website at www.gsea.org.

Instruction Manual Available
to Teacher of Entrepreneurship

This book can be used as a text
for middle school, high school, or college students
interested in entrepreneurship

To receive a free copy of the instruction manual log on to
www.gsea.org.